FREEDOM'S RUSH

Foster Kinn

HUGO HOUSE PUBLISHERS, LTD.

Freedom's Rush, by Foster Kinn

ISBN: 978-1-936449-28-6

Library of Congress Control Number: 2013949621

Cover design: NZ Graphics

Interior Design: Taylor by Design

Cover Photo: Dwight Mikkelsen

Hugo House Publishers
Denver, Colorado
Austin, Texas
www.HugoHousePublishers.com

CONTENTS

This book is dedicated to the three best kids in the world:
Khalin, Lacee, and Jasmine
(Or, as I like to call them, The Good Man, Sweetness, and Twinkle)

and, of course,
Rosemary

PREFACE

I didn't start out to write a book. What I did start out to do was ride. Just that. I wanted to ride my motorcycle, travel on roads I'd never before traveled, meet people I'd never before met, see things I'd never before seen. Breathe a different air.

When I left on my first multi-day trip, my kids were understandably a little worried. Here's their dad riding off, alone, on a motorcycle with no schedule, no motel reservations, no particular destinations and no specific routes in mind. I told them I'd write regular emails so they'd know I was okay. I figured my close friends would also want to know that I was okay so I sent the emails to them, too.

At first, these emails were short, but the more miles I covered the more creative I got, which meant they got longer and more detailed. Soon, I was including photos and calling them TravelBlogs. During the same time, more and more people asked to be on the mailing list so, of course, I added them. And it continued like that: The list of recipients grew right along with the TravelBlogs.

Though the TravelBlogs became longer, I tried keeping them under fifteen hundred words, which meant that I had to leave out many of the things that had happened. During the 2011 holidays I took a fresh look at all those TravelBlogs and, for just the fun of it, began filling in the things that I had originally left out. It was only then that I started creating this book, though it took some weeks before I realized it. I mean, before that, sure, I'd *thought* of writing a book but now I was actually *doing* it. After two rides in 2012, one during the summer and the other during the autumn, I had finally visited all the states in the western half of the continental United States and was finally ready to finish *Freedom's Rush*.

It would be impossible to give adequate thanks to Andrew Surina and the rest of the guys at Fire Breathing Industries, who made my bike the beast he is, and never fail to keep him tip-top. The supremely literate Patricia Ross did, as you would expect, a supreme job of editing and I thank her for being patient with my boneheadedness. Chelsea Cohen topped it off with an equally supreme job of proofreading. Nick Zelinger, a genius, did the exemplary cover and Ronda Taylor, another genius, did the exemplary formatting and included all my last-minute amendments without a peep of protest. Also, thanks to my old pal Dwight Mikkelsen for the photos. Truly, none of the people mentioned above could have been paid too much. And a shout out to my wonderful family and friends who patiently waited for all my photo-laden emails to download, took the time to read them, and send back emails thanking me.

Last, I acknowledge and thank everyone who has, at least once, done something for Freedom. Freedom, my friends, is the wellspring of all triumphs, great and beautiful and joyous.

BIKERS' ANTHEM

We ride.

It's in our sinews, our marrows, our pulsing bloods;
Our cellular codes, our breathings, our touchings.

We ride over mountains and through valleys,
Around parks and towns,
Into and out of our dreams.

We ride with music blasting
Or in that magnetic mix of wind and engine rumble.
We ride with windshields or without,
With helmets or without,
With friends or strangers or alone.

We ride in sunshine and moonless nights;
Through high winds, rain, snow and hail.
We ride on freeways, highways and parkways;
On side roads, back roads, dirt roads, on no roads at all.

We ride to the familiar and to the new,
To anywhere and everywhere,
To hidden-, forgotten- and lost-wheres.

We ride to get away, we ride to get to,
We ride for no reason at all;
It is our history, our future, our now.

As long as freedoms exist, we will ride;
As long as we ride, freedoms will exist.

THE BEAST

Motorcycles. Let me say that again. Motorcycles.

I love motorcycles and everything about them. The look, the smell, the feel, the greasy dirt, the sound, everything. Oddly, however, not everyone feels the same. For some reason, there are people who don't like the feel and smell of greasy dirt or the sound of an engine revving. Further, some people see them as a threat. To others, they represent danger. To some, they're a symbol of lawlessness, irresponsibility and debauchery. Then there are those who think they're just another hunk of metal. But to the rest of us, they're something else entirely.

To us, it is a fact that motorcycles are alive. Each has its own personality, its own way of doing things, its own likes and dislikes. (For instance, I once rode a Harley Road King that, I swear, hated my guts.) Like the rest of us, they have good days and bad days, and if you listen closely, they'll let you know what kind of day it is. (Now that I write that, maybe that Road King was just in a bad mood that day.)

Motorcycles are either male, female or some a combination of both. Whatever the gender, some of them seem more alive than others, but I think the reason has much more to do with the rider than with the bike. It is true that if you say something to your bike, he or she (or they) will respond. This is why you never truly ride alone. It's a blessing because you can be some place where the closest human is a hundred miles away, yet a good conversation is right there, riding along with you. If you've never spoken with a bike, I'll offer a cautionary word: A bike will always tell you the full truth, even if it's a brutal one.

Right before we take off on any trip, short or long, I always tell my bike, "Let's do this right." He always responds, "The way it's supposed to be done."

The following chapters chronicle the freedoms of five multi-day rides throughout the western half of the continental United States, a handful of day-rides, and a side trip into Central Canada. Before I get to them, I should tell you a little about my faithful companion, The Beast, who accompanied me every inch of those thirty-thousand-plus miles. I must admit that he managed all those miles – the weather, the roads, the traffic, all of it – far better than me.

The Beast and I first met back in July of 2009. At the time, I was riding a Yamaha V-Star 650, which I really liked, and still do, but I wanted a bigger bike. I'd never ridden a Harley before but figured I would get a used one and try it out for a while. If I didn't like it, I could always resell it in six months and not lose much money, if any. There was even a chance I'd make money because motorcycles hold their value well after their first year.

I looked at and tried out a number of Softail Deuces and Softail Standards, the two models that most appealed to me, and I would have been happy with almost any of them. However, there was one who, for several reasons, stood out from the others, not the least of which was that he wore the two most proper colors for a motorcycle: black and chrome. But the thing that grabbed me the most happened when I first saw him.

He was sitting on a driveway covered with dust and a "for sale" sign. Just quietly sitting right there. But there was a smoldering under the dust, as if he was waiting for a chance to roar, a chance to explode down a freeway, a chance to feel his pegs carve deep ruts into canyon roads. My first impression was that he was a beast.

A week later, I ponied up the money, got his pink slip and we headed home, our first real ride together. The first thing we encountered was some radical road construction and it took a full thirty minutes to go the ten miles to the 605 Freeway. It was not fun. There wasn't even ten feet of smooth road surface and because he was so different from my Yamaha, I was not handling him well. I felt like a newborn horse on its legs for the first time. When I got onto the 605, my attention was completely absorbed by the hostile traffic and the awkward way I was navigating through it. Then, nine miles later, on the long turn onto the 210 Freeway West, the traffic became sparse and I could finally put all my attention on just riding. The space around us extended out for miles, and the unique thrill of riding my new Harley Softail Deuce hit me deep down.

We quickly got used to each other and within a few days we were as comfortable as if we'd been riding together for ten years. At the time, he didn't have a name but I wanted to give him one so I listed out a half-dozen options ("The Beast" was not one of them) and spent the next five days deciding which I liked the best. I finally decided on "The Babe" and did so for only one reason: I thought it would make for a funny line. If someone asked how I was doing, I could say, "Great! Just ridin' The Babe all day every day." It is a pretty funny line, I guess, but it came with a cost.

I told him his name the following weekend during a ride to the California coast with my buddy, Vic. I immediately began having problems. The twisties on Highway 38 in the Coastal Range became impossible to negotiate; my line of travel on the turns was either too sharp or too wide and I often ended up on the shoulder, once almost colliding with a pickup coming the other way. Try as I might, there was no way I could keep up with Vic, even though he was on a big Kawasaki touring bike, which he claims "handles like a pig in mud." (It's really not like that at all.) My sudden lack of expertise was too embarrassing to admit, even to myself, and one time I actually pulled over to photograph some cows, hoping it would disguise the fact that I was riding like a newbie and couldn't keep up a respectable speed.

When we got off of the 101 Freeway in Atascadero, I turned so wide that I ended up in the weeds and the car behind me had to wait while I backed up onto the asphalt. When I pulled into the gas station, I bumped the pump island with my front tire and almost fell down. And wouldn't you know it, right next to me was a young, sexy woman on a Suzuki sport bike. She shook her head in disgust.

When I went to park in front of the convenience store, I turned too sharply and fell down. My right leg was folded under "The Babe", my left leg was on top of it and there was simply no way for me to get it upright. Vic was already in the store so I had no one to help me but a gangling teenager drinking a forty-four ounce cup of something or other. At first he put his left hand on the higher handgrip as if he was going to pull up the bike as easily as he would his empty backpack. (His right hand was still fiercely clutching his forty-four-ouncer.) I said, "Look, that's not going to work. This thing weighs seven hundred pounds and I have no leverage. It may break my knee but I'll be damned if it's going to touch the ground." I had him put down his drink, come over to the low side, and after a fair amount of grunting we managed to push "The Babe" onto the kickstand.

I was in a state of confusion and disbelief, and wandered up and down the convenience store aisles for a few minutes trying to figure out what was wrong. Why was I all of a sudden so clumsy? Finally it hit me: he must hate his name! I needed to apologize and come up with a new one, one that was actually fitting. And I needed to do it fast or I'd end up going down permanently. I thought back to when we first met and there was only one choice. I went out, apologized, then announced that his name was, now and forever, The Beast. Since then, we've been problem free.

Except for two accidents. But neither was the fault of The Beast. On each, I fell prey to what is possibly the foremost undoing of all bikers: inattention. The first accident resulted in a broken left ankle, a broken left foot, a broken finger and two forearms covered with serious road rash. I was in a wheel chair and on crutches for four months and my left ankle will forever host a stainless steel plate and six screws. The second accident resulted in a busted right knee, a broken right shinbone and another broken finger. Again I couldn't ride for four months.

Despite all that, I never once entertained the idea of never riding again. As soon as I was physically able to kick up the gear shifter and step on the brake, we got back to putting in the miles, The Beast and I, and we put in a lot.

The Beast has gotten a lot of modifications since we first met and every one made him better, better in all ways, and after each accident, he had expert bodywork done just as I had my operations and rehab. It's interesting. Though he's nothing but black and chrome, along with a few dark silver pinstripes, he gets at least as many compliments as any bike with a special paint job. As I've said many times, The Beast looks like, sounds like and rides like a motorcycle is supposed to. Today, he continues to run and rumble and turn heads in admiration.

Some day, I'll get another bike and ride that one for a lot of miles, too. But I'll never part with The Beast. We share too much history to do that, history that is chronicled in all our scratches, scrapes, scars and worn spots, the inevitable hallmarks of hard riding. And we wear those imperfections proudly because they're *ours*, proof that we've stayed together all this time.

3

PERSPECTIVES

Evidently, I chose the wrong time to ride south out of Madison, Wisconsin. I'm on Interstate 39 in the northwestern corner of Illinois and the traffic is crazy. Monumentally crazy. The kind of crazy where you can't find a safe line of travel, where you wish you were riding a fully armed Batman bike, where you feel like you're in one of those video games with all the alien spaceships coming right at you and all you have is the skill to play a decent game of Ms. Pacman. However, there is one other thing I do notice: Something like eighty percent of the road signs have to do with Chicago. But they don't help me at all because I'm not going to Chicago. My plan is to get into Iowa. So I bravely brave the crazy craziness and stop only once for gas.

Early in the evening, I get a room in Davenport, Iowa that's close to some fast food joints, the reason being that once I unload everything, I don't want to have to ride very far to get dinner. In fact, I'd rather walk at that point. I tell the guy at the motel desk my three preferences for a room: bottom floor, wireless signal, and cheap. He mentions that the weekend before there was an antique motorcycle show in town and wants to know why it is that *every* biker wanted a room on the bottom floor. I explain the relationship between a rider and his bike, that you want it close by so you can keep an eye on it, that a motorcycle is a personal thing, that there is a fast attachment between bike and biker. He's not getting it. He says that damage and theft is what insurance is for, that you can always get another motorcycle, so why worry about it. I tell him,

"It's like that old cowboy philosophy: Steal his wife and he'll get a little upset, steal his horse and he'll kill you."

The next day I get an early start, going west on Interstate 80. It's cold. I'm bent forward and not shifting around, trying to conserve my body heat. The slate-like clouds are heavy and low-lying, and there is no echo at all from my engine. The direct rains have transformed the sweeping cornfields into a sanctuary of deep saffron and glowing green, and I'm in the mood to see it all as an endless array of ancient, moss-covered statues of forgotten saints on a velvet carpet. A sheltered tranquility. It's one of those times, one of those stretches of riding, when it's more like you're simply *being* there rather than riding-through.

I pull off the freeway but not for gas. I just want a cup of hot chocolate to warm up the innards. I end up talking on the phone with one of my kids and right after the I-love-yous, get on The Beast and take off. It's raining harder now and a few miles later, a double-trailer truck passes me. (Okay, maybe I'm exaggerating a little, but, I swear, in the Midwest, double-trailer trucks must have a *minimum* speed limit of 90 mph.) As he passes, he honks and points to the back of my bike so I twist around to look. The big round case on my luggage rack is open and the right flap is flapping around like a newborn sparrow in a tornado.

I pull over and assess my losses: night glasses, a pair of fingerless gloves, two t-shirts (one of them new), two pairs of dirty socks, a bottle of water, and a bunch of other things I'd stuffed in there. When I close up the case I realize I had left my keys on top of it back at the hot chocolate stop, which means they went flying off in the wind, which means that my handy Swiss Army knife, a flash drive, and the key that locks my bike are gone as well.

I know it's futile but I retrace my route anyway. I see nothing. Except for rain-soaked pavement and ninety mile-per-hour double-trailer trucks. The magic happens a little over a year later. I'm actually working on this very chapter. I'd already written it so all I was doing was sprucing it up; things like making sure I didn't write 'of' instead of 'if', or didn't write 'the' twice in a row, stuff like that. I take a break, go to the bedroom to get my phone and see that I have a voicemail from someone named Molly. She says her car broke down on the I-80 west of Davenport and while she was waiting for the tow truck, she sees a flash drive lying on the shoulder and it turns out that it's the very same one I'd lost over a year ago in the cold rain.

This is amazing. It sat on the shoulder of Interstate 80 for over a year in the rain, the snow and the hot sun, and the wind never blew it off into the weeds. Then an Iowan angel sees it (what are the chances?), takes it home, goes through all the trouble of cleaning it, finds out it still works (it still works!), finds a document with my name on it, and then contacts me. So I call Molly-the-Iowan-Angel and she offers to mail it to me. What a sweet, sweet lady!

Getting back to Interstate 80, the hard rain, the bracing cold, and hot-footed truck drivers.

I pull over to get gas in Coralville, which is on the west side of Iowa City, and spot the Hawkeye Harley Dealership a couple of blocks away. I ride over and buy a black t-shirt on the front of which is written "Ride Free, Ride Hard, Ride Often." I walk out the front door and start a conversation with Mike and Dwight, two bikers from Northern Iowa, and they tell me that the last Iowa Bike Night of the year is that very night in Indianola. I ask Mike if Indianola is a big city and he says, "Oh yeah, it's big. There must be, oh, fifteen thousand people livin' there." It takes a few moments for me to grasp the concept of a population of fifteen thousand as being big, or even qualifying as a city and not a town. I mean, I live in Southern California, which, population-wise, seems endless. For instance, Glendale (the one in California, not Arizona) has a population of over two hundred thousand but is so swallowed up in the Los Angeles effluvium that you can't even tell where the city limits are. Nevertheless, I raise my eyebrows and nod in mild wonder.

I get back on the I-80 and continue west toward my next stop, which is Omaha. After a short while it occurs to me: What! I'd be crazy to miss Indianola Bike Night! I'm pretty sure it's somewhere southwest but have no idea how far it is or how to get there. Nevertheless, I pull off the freeway and go south for a while. I figure I'll stop and ask for directions and there won't be any problems. Indianola is a big city, right? Everyone must know how to get there, right? I can't miss it, right? Besides, I've a hankering to see the Iowa countryside.

I ride the Iowa countryside and it's easy and fun. From what I see, it's covered with prosperous farms, there's an occasional silo made of multi-colored bricks, and every ten to twenty miles is a clean, shady, comfortable little town with a gas station, a firehouse, a church or two, a park, a museum, and a library. Much of the time the roads are pretty straight but the rest of the time you're either leaning easily or going up and down like a horse on an easy merry-go-round. To give you an idea how much I like it, the map says the distance from Coralville to Indianola is 126 miles. I log well over two hundred.

My route is so odd and jagged that it looks like I was drunk on corn whiskey when I planned it. I stop and ask for directions in Wayland where it seems like one of the pastimes is cultivating healthy lawns. Really, I don't see one that's in need of care. I head west for a while then go north and stop in Sigourney for more directions. The ladies at the gas station mini-market are sitting on the floor trying to fix one of the refrigerator units. They ask if I know anything about fixing refrigerator units, which, regrettably, I don't, so I offer to lift anything heavy, which is something I'm pretty good at, but they're all set in that department. I head west, then north at Delta and pass through What Cheer and wonder about the story behind the name. I go west again at Deep River, south at Montezuma (more directions), then west one more time through New Sharon and into Pella, where I decide to gas up and find a Dairy Queen.

There's road construction just outside of Pella and I'm diverted through a downtown neighborhood and it's one of the prettiest towns I've ever seen. Turns out it has the largest working windmill in the United States, is the site of an annual tulip festival, and was Wyatt Earp's boyhood home. I find my Dairy Queen on Oskaloosa Street and while I'm waiting for my 1/3 pound GrillBurger, I ask the young fellow behind the counter for directions to Indianola. He's a little impatient because I'd interrupted his flirting with the two girls who are his fellow Dairy Queen employees, so he calls over the manager and she gives me directions. A slice of American life.

I head out to my bike with the directions swimming around in my head. At the bottom of the hill do I turn right at the stop sign? Or do I go straight at the stop sign and turn right at the next big road? Or is it a left turn? And what was I supposed to do when I see the big white farmhouse? It doesn't matter, I think, there's still an hour or so of daylight left and Indianola is a big city, right? Everyone knows where it is, right? I can't miss it, right?

Before I start up the engine I look around. Behind me is a modest, quiet neighborhood with tree-lined streets; in front of me the traffic on Oskaloosa Street is easy and courteous. In the parking lot is an old, yellow Dodge Charger alongside a Chevy Chevelle covered with primer, which is alongside an old Ford pickup. I look at those three vehicles and it strikes me that I am truly in the heart of America, and it is a fine feeling. Tell you what, my friends, if you ever have a chance, go to Pella, Iowa. I'm certain you'll come away feeling the same.

Not far outside of Pella, I cross over the Des Moines River, a tranquil artery in America's heart, where I spend quite a while taking photos. Once I get close to Bike Night, Indianola is easy to find. Just follow the other bikers! It's smack dab in the middle of town and fills the block surrounding the brick courthouse. The only parking space I can find is on a small side street where, a little ways away, three easy-going Indianola policemen are having a chat. I go over.

Me: Say, you fellas think my bike will be safe over there? (I point)

Easy-Going Indianola Policeman: (Looking as if it's the most off-the-wall question he's ever heard) Safe?

Me: Yeah. Do you think it's an okay place to park?

Easy-Going Indianola Policeman: (Still perplexed) Well, why wouldn't it be okay to park there?

Me: (Just now thinking about what are probably vastly different crime statistics between downtown Indianola, Iowa and downtown Los Angeles, California) Oh, I don't know. It's just that I'm from Southern California and we have to, you know, be careful where we park.

Easy-Going Indianola Policeman: (Looking as if he's been introduced to a new and odd concept) You have to be careful where you park in Southern California?

Me: Oh yeah. You know, big cities and all that. Stuff happens.

Easy-Going Indianola Policeman: (Nods slowly, finally understanding my concern) Oh, you don't have anything to worry about. You just go on and have a good time.

Indianola Bike Night. There's a live band (a good one!), people are walking their dogs, children are dancing, everyone nods and smiles, and many ask how I'm doing. There are about three hundred bikes with all sorts of different paint jobs, from black on black to hot pink on pink. Vendors are selling handmade jewelry (I buy a ten dollar ring for my left pinky), locally designed t-shirts (I had to have one), vests, jackets, chaps, wallets, and keychains. There are raffle tickets for the animal shelter (I buy a dozen and give them to a mother and daughter) and places to get temporary and permanent tattoos. For dinner, there are corn dogs, several different kinds of barbecue (all spicy hot), pulled pork sandwiches, tri-tip walking tacos, ribs, and beef and chili bowls. I get the feeling that the nearest vegetable is sitting on a dark, lonely shelf in Des Moines, so this is my kind of place.

I see my new friends, Mike and Dwight, and meet their wives, Mary and Kathy. I'm still excited about my ride through the prosperous southern Iowa countryside. I tell them how lucky they are to live in Iowa, that the roads are fun, that the Des Moines River is fabulous and makes for great photos, and that the easily rolling roads are among the most fun in America. Mike, a long distance truck driver from northern Iowa, cocks his head and says, "Well, North Iowa ain't like that; it's all pretty much flat and straight."

We chat for a while and I make them promise to ride out to Southern California some summer so I can show them our legendary canyons. I tell them about Angeles Crest's sixty miles of perfectly designed road with glorious scenery, about Lockwood Valley Road and the renowned Highway 33, which are much the same. About the beautiful views on Angeles Forest, the trio of Tujungas (Little, Big and Upper Big), Bouquet Canyon, Spunky Canyon and San Francisquito Canyon. About Mount Baldy and Glendora Ridge, how you can see clear across the San Gabriel Valley on one side or down into the two pristine lakes on the other. About The Rim of the World Highway and Highway 138 that goes through the Valley of Enchantment where the air is so fresh it can cure asthma and bronchitis. (Hey, I'm on a PR roll!) About City Creek Road, how you ride it to Highway 18 and at the end of Big Bear Lake you go south on Highway 38 straight through the lush San Bernardino National Forest. And that's just some of the great riding *north* of Los Angeles. South of Los Angeles is a whole other world.

Even though it's a Friday, Indianola Bike Night starts to shut down around nine o'clock and it's all over by ten. Good times. I ride north into Des Moines and get a good night's sleep.

The next morning, I get a late start. It's still cold and raining. Really cold and really raining. I pull into a truck stop a little while after the chill becomes painful. (You know the saying: There's cold, then there's motorcycle cold.) I go straight to the bathroom and warm my hands under the hot air hand dryer and in my current condition I'm thinking it's one of the greatest inventions ever. I buy a cup of hot chocolate then stand outside under the eave to conduct an experiment. I want to find out if it's possible to be in temperature like this, totally soaked, and not shiver. It also gives me time to ponder my two choices: keep riding in the freezing rain and be a fool, or get a motel room, wait for the storms to pass and be a wimp. What I'm *really* doing, of course, is trying to figure out which is the lesser indignity: being a fool or being a wimp. So there I am, pondering my fate, when a fellow walks out of the store, pauses to look at me and The Beast, then goes to his truck. He's about to get in when he steps back, closes the door and walks over. It's then that I'm introduced to the understated humor that's characteristic of the Midwest.

Midwestern Trucker Fellow: I'd say you're a braver man than me, riding a motorcycle in weather like this.

Me: Funny, I was thinking I wasn't quite as smart.

Midwestern Trucker Fellow: *(Grins, nods, raises his eyebrows)* Well …

I go back in and get another cup of hot chocolate and ask the young woman behind the counter where I am. She says I'm in Omaha. "Really?" I say, "I'm already in Nebraska?" She's not surprised at all and just nods and asks, "Where ya headed?" I tell her I'm just going to ride through Nebraska, maybe take a couple of side roads. She tells me I'll hate it. "Why?" I ask. "It's all flat, nuthin's there. You'll hate it."

I decide that being a fool is more dignified than being a wimp, so I start my ride through Nebraska's cold rain and, despite the prediction of the young woman in Omaha, I rather enjoy it. Sometimes you need a broad, unobstructed view for things to settle out, at which time you can ponder the important issues of life, like would it be possible to make money by designing and selling earrings with little battery-powered heaters in them.

I stop for the night in Lincoln and am immediately convinced that the only two colors of clothes in Lincoln are scarlet and cream, the school colors of the University of Nebraska at Lincoln. The next day is Saturday. Game day. A home game day. And the football stadium is right down the street. Everyone, and I mean *everyone*, in and around the motel (except yours truly) is wearing scarlet and cream that has something about the Nebraska Cornhuskers football team written on it. Heck, even the motel is on Cornhusker Highway. Note that it's not something small like an avenue or street or road. It's a *highway*. I'd bet that if aliens in a spaceship took a photo of the United States during a Cornhuskers home game, they'd wonder for weeks about the big patch of scarlet and cream right in the middle.

Caught up in all the football fever around me (the Cornhuskers won, by the way) I figure I'll take a day off from riding and spend all Sunday watching NFL games on TV. It sounds like a good idea, and it is, but it doesn't work out. Around two o' clock I'm antsy to get back on the road, which I would have done had I not already paid for the room for another night. I do get on the bike, however, and set about riding around the outskirts of Lincoln.

Over the years I have found that one of the best techniques, if not the best, for learning your way around a new area is to go out, get lost, then find your way back. I'm out, only partly lost, when I come upon Conestoga Lake, where I find a perfect spot for photos only to discover that my camera is back in the motel room. With sunset quickly approaching, I take off, find my way back and grab my camera. But because I now know my way around, I get back to Conestoga Lake just in time to catch a mind-blowing sunset.

The fellow at the motel desk was a little gruff when I had spoken with him earlier but I nevertheless got the impression he was basically a friendly guy. Brimming with satisfaction over my ability to find my way in time to catch that sunset, I decide to start up a conversation. Turns out my impression was right, he is a friendly guy. His gruffness comes from the fact that he grew up way out in the countryside and doesn't like the fact that there are now so many people in Nebraska. He feels the state he loves has become over-crowded, that living there has become a cramped existence.

I think about Nebraska's mellow ambience, quiet satisfaction and lack of arrogance; about its wide-open countryside and infinite skies; about the completely unencumbered rides I've enjoyed while here. Even in and around Lincoln and Omaha I never came close to anything resembling a traffic jam. I compare all of that with where I live, with being one of tens of thousands on the 405 Freeway in Southern California on a Friday afternoon driving along at a walking pace; with spending forty-five minutes maneuvering my way out of the Hollywood Bowl parking lot after a Saturday night concert; with taking an hour to find a parking space at the Glendale Galleria on Christmas Eve. I look at him and say, "Yeah, I know what you mean."

By morning the rain has stopped and the air is about as clean as air can get. And it's not nearly as cold. I continue on Interstate 80 West and take more side trips through a comforting, colorful landscape crisscrossed with rivers and creeks. I get a couple of views of the Platte River, and the North Platte and the South Platte, too, and each time have an urge to know more about their histories. (The three rivers Platt often crop up in the stories of the Plains Indians and the Pioneers.) As the young woman in Omaha claimed, it's all pretty much flat. There are no mountains or even hills, really, just an occasional grass-covered hummock and a lot of corn. Still I don't mind. The land is dotted with lakes and ponds and pretty yellow butterflies dancing around like they're giddy in paradise, which to them, they probably are.

I pull into a rest area next to the Platte River. Next to the parking area is a large, blue plastic trashcan that gives me a chuckle. Embossed on the lid are the words RICKY RECEPTACLE SAYS THANK YOU! This particular rest area has what amounts to a miniature museum, so I walk on in and give myself a miniature tour. I like reading the informative signs in rest areas, which are like miniature histories with fun facts. Like Nebraska came from the word *Nebraskier*, which was a French version of an Otoe Indian word for "flat." And "Platte" comes from the old French word *plat*, which also means flat. Who knew?

I go for a short walk along the Platte and come across a sizable, perfectly defined, stainless steel sculpture that's sitting in the smoothly flowing waters. Just sitting right there. It's an odd sight and at first I don't like it. Well, it's not so much that I dislike the sculpture, I dislike the fact that it is where it is, a modern, perfectly defined steel sculpture in the middle of the ancient Platte with its irregular banks, tall grasses, dancing yellow butterflies and rich history. But because it's an odd sight, I decide I want a photo of it, so I walk around looking for a good angle.

After getting my photo (which is quite good, thank you very much) I stand there a while thinking. When he was commissioned, the sculptor, George Baker, obviously had a different perspective, a different idea of beauty than something that would blend in with the natural beauty of the Platte River. In a metaphorical way, his sculpture is similar to me: a Californian from the Los Angeles metropolitan area, wandering around the Heartland of America. On more than a few accounts, I don't fit in. I'm an outsider just like Mr. Baker's stainless steel sculpture. Now, the fact that I am an outsider doesn't make me in any way wrong or unwelcome, only different. Besides, I like being here. I take another look at Mr. Baker's sculpture and now I like it. I not only like it, I like how it sits there, calmly and without apology, the same way I'm standing on the banks of the Platte in America's Heartland.

On the other side of the proverbial coin are the many, many things all of us *do* have in common, differences in ancestry, religions, political affiliations, ages, and mores notwithstanding. And one of those commonalities is humor. As a side note: I once looked up "comedy" and "humor" in a thesaurus dictionary. The similarity is that they both point out something illogical or absurd and are intended to get a laugh. The difference is that, by definition, humor is kind, comedy not necessarily so. Those in the Midwest seem to know this difference instinctively and are natural masters of humor, which is another reason I like it here.

The thing is, humor demands more cleverness and insight, more thought, than comedy. It's also a more comfortable setting for wit and irony. For instance, say there's an unshaven, unkempt group of guys (you know, like bikers) and an uppity woman sneers in disgust when she walks by. One of the guys says, "My kind of slut." Not very clever but it might get a laugh. On the other hand, in the same scenario one of them says, "Ah! It is the east, and Juliet is the sun!"

I have a few one-liners I've been saying for years and years. Why? Because most times they get a chuckle. There's an unwritten law in comedy and humor: If it keeps getting laughs, keep using it. (Think

Henny Youngman and "Take my wife. Please," or Rodney Dangerfield and "I don't get no respect.") Now, I like getting chuckles out of people but it's especially satisfying when they're quick-witted enough to go along with one of my mini-shticks.

I walk into another cheap motel, this one in North Platte. When I'm not sleeping on the ground (not something I often do) I almost always stay in a cheap motel. In fact, some of these places are so cheap that when I finally check into something equivalent to a Motel 6, I feel like I'm in the uppermost suite in that ridiculously tall hotel in Dubai. Dang, hot water and a heater that works!

Anyway, as I was saying, I'm in North Platte and walk into another cheap motel. The lady behind the desk is, well, large. Majestically large. And she wears her largeness proudly, like a badge of accomplishment, and she wears her wrinkled Mother Hubbard like it's the latest style from Paris.

Majestically Large Cornhusker Desk Lady: That'll be $27.21, including tax.

Me: That comes with a free car wash, right?

Majestically Large Cornhusker Desk Lady: *(No hesitation)* Of course.

Me: By a supermodel in a thong and roller skates?

Majestically Large Cornhusker Desk Lady: Oh I'm sorry, today's her day off. *(Winks)* But I got a bikini that'll set ya thinkin' everything's right.

Me: Sounds good!

Majestically Large Cornhusker Desk Lady: But then a few of my boyfriends might get jealous. And you don't want that kind of trouble. *(Winks again)*

4

BLESSINGS

We shall not cease from exploration
And the end of all our exploring
Will be to arrive where we started
And know the place for the first time.

—T.S. Eliot

California is a beautiful state. True, you can say that about every state in the union but because I've lived in California all my life and am intimate with much of its beauty, I make that statement with authority. The blessed beaches that look out over the endless peace of the Pacific Ocean, the Sierra Nevada Mountains that are like spires atop Mother Nature's cathedral, the Giant Redwoods that radiate like proud and benevolent gods, the implacable Mojave Desert that reminds us of a different kind of god.

I'd been working pretty hard and steadily for a while. It was all good (I needed the money) but it got to a point where I wanted a reprieve, I *needed* a reprieve, a reprieve that wouldn't interrupt my income. I get the good news on a Wednesday afternoon in mid-Summer: a week postponement. Yes! I pack that night and the next morning I head north on Interstate 5, also known as the Golden State Freeway. Because I've traveled countless, uneventful miles on this freeway and know the San

Joaquin Valley so well, I was not expecting this to be the start of one of my most memorable rides.

It's a sad fact that one of the few routes in California that has never inspired me is the I-5 from the Los Angeles area through the mountains of Los Padres National Forest to the San Joaquin Valley. I don't know if the reason is that I've traveled it hundreds of times so it's difficult to view it with fresh eyes, or because it's simply not an inspiring stretch of freeway. Or maybe it's the fact that most of those trips were done in a car so I was never *really in* the environment, never really looking. Or maybe it's because traveling on an eight-lane superslab while avoiding slow-moving trucks and sports cars darting about like they're qualifying for the Daytona 500 is not conducive to enjoying your surroundings. Whatever the reason, for me it's long since been nothing more than the first sixty-some-odd miles I pass through as quickly as possible on my way to Visalia (vie-SAIL-ya), my home town.

The only remarkable sight I've ever seen along this route was courtesy of world-renowned artists Christo and his wife Jeanne-Claude. Together, they create enormous, temporary artscapes that cover acres and acres and are free for public viewing. In October 1991, they covered the area around Tejon Ranch, where it borders the I-5, with large yellow umbrellas, at the same time covering a similar area in Japan with large blue umbrellas. It was delightful. I went there with a friend and my younger daughter and we spent hours walking around. It's interesting because other than walking around, there was nothing to actually do. No rides, no tours, no games, nothing. Just a bunch of big yellow umbrellas. Yet we were happy to spend hours just being there.

I sincerely admire what Christo and his wife Jeanne-Claude create, that they have the good manners to always clean up after themselves, and that they're willing to put up with legions of bureaucrats and mountains of red tape in order to do what they do. But what I especially admire is the fact that, as artists, they are completely free from any outside influence, as all real artists are. They accept no grants, sponsorships, subsidies or royalties; they endorse no products, no businesses, no political or social movements, or anything else. As Cristo himself has said, "We wish to work in total freedom." Freedom. I love that word.

Other than the temporary yellow umbrellas artscape, there's one other spot I should mention. It's about five miles north of Lebec and when you're going north and the skies are clear, which isn't often the case, the mountains slowly open up to reveal the San Joaquin Valley grandly stretching forever into the distance.

Right before coming out of the mountains, the I-5 splits left and right at what's called the Grapevine. For years I'd assumed it was called that because if you apply a little imagination while looking at a map, each side of the freeway resembles a grapevine. But the truth is a little more straightforward. Wild grapes had been growing in that area and it had been called the Grapevine for decades before President Eisenhower persuaded Congress to build our system of interstate freeways. (So much for imagination.) Three miles after the Grapevine is Wheeler Ridge, which is composed of two sprawling restaurant/gas/fast food/rest areas, one for each side of the freeway, and it's usually my only stop.

A mile later the I-5 veers a little more to the northwest, but I continue straight north on US Highway 99. At this point, the I-5 is still the Golden State Freeway but the 99 becomes the Golden State Highway, though I've never heard anyone refer to it as that. To those of us who grew up in the San Joaquin Valley it was always just "the 99." Despite its highway moniker, the 99 from the Grapevine to Sacramento *is* a freeway; a mostly-straight and mostly-boring freeway that doesn't offer any worthwhile views except on clear days when you can see the Sierra Nevada Mountains far to the east. However, it's a better ride than the I-5, which is even more straight and boring.

Some years ago, someone pointed out an interesting difference between east coast and west coast terminology when referring to numbered highways and roads. Those on the east coast generally don't use the article "the" before the number. They'll say, "Take 99 north." We on the west coast will insert "the" and say, "Take the 99 north." Even as a west coaster, I admit that our use of "the" is inconsistent. For instance, in the second paragraph above I wrote, "I head north on Interstate 5," but in the very next paragraph I wrote, "… the I-5 from the Los Angeles area…." For some reason, shortening "Interstate 5" to "I-5" makes me want to insert the word "the" and I can't come up with a grammatical reason why. But we west coasters have always done it and will most likely keep on doing it. Perhaps it's a way to claim our roots.

I pass through Bakersfield, the western bastion of country music. (There are even streets called Merle Haggard Drive and Buck Owens

Boulevard.) Over the years, Bakersfield has been the target of, to put it mildly, many unfavorable comments, including some from yours truly. Honestly however, they're mostly undeserved, except for the pervasive petroleum smell during summer, which is due to the fact than Kern County is the highest oil-producing county in the United States, and yields more crude oil than the entire state of Oklahoma. Despite the petroleum smell, the local citizenry does a fine job of creating a unique and worthwhile city, especially when you consider that it sits in the middle of a semi-arid desert. In fact, if it weren't for irrigation the entire San Joaquin Valley would still be a semi-arid desert.

After Bakersfield are the towns of Famoso, McFarland, Delano, Earlimart, Pixley, and Tipton. (We pronounce Delano "duh-LAY-no" and not "DEL-uh-no," which is the acceptable pronunciation when saying Franklin Delano Roosevelt.) The smaller of these, along with a few others set well away from the 99, are functional places: a market or two, a church or two, a diner or two, an elementary school, a gas station, a tack and feed store, a library, a fire station, and a couple of policemen. Earlimart and Delano are the two largest towns so they actually have high schools. Whatever the population, these towns do a good job of fulfilling the needs of the good rural folks.

South of Tulare (tuh-LAIR-ee), I pull off at Paige Avenue, take a back way to Mooney Boulevard, ride into Visalia and have lunch at Ryan's Place. I'm finishing the last of my fries when the friendly waitress gives me a free piece of berry pie. I say, "Ah! It's a piece of berry pie!" She smiles and says, "Just thought you'd enjoy it, Darlin'." If you think it through, this is a sound business practice (wish every place did it!) because from now on, whenever I go to Visalia, I'll eat at Ryan's Place. Plus, whenever a waitress gives me a free piece of pie, my tip amount doubles, and I tip well to begin with.

I'm chewing the last bit of pie when she bends over to pick up something she "accidentally" dropped, and I'm treated to a close-up view of the female version of the Grand Canyon. I triple my tip.

After lunch, I ride over to my boyhood home east of Lovers Lane. The huge oak tree at the end of our street was cut down years ago and the vast fields to the east are now covered with closely placed homes. The outside of the house I grew up in is now paneled and painted blue which, admittedly, looks much better than the faded orange stucco it was when I was a kid. I also ride by Mineral King Elementary School, where I attended kindergarten through eighth grade, and my beloved Mt. Whitney High School, where I spent four fun-filled years. It's dismaying that the school officials found it necessary to surround each school with a tall, chain-link fence with locked gates. Perhaps this is a side product of a growing population: It was fifteen to twenty thousand when I was a kid and it's around one hundred forty thousand now. Just once, I wish I could see it all the way it originally was.

I take the 198 Freeway seven miles west to the trusty 99 and continue north to Fresno, my ultimate destination. Why Fresno? Well, I'm writing a novel and most of it takes place in that city. I haven't been there in years and I want to ride around and get a feel for it so that my writing will be authentic. (Besides, it's only an hour away from Yosemite.) I get to Fresno and find a cheap motel on Blackstone Avenue. There are still several hours of sunlight left so I take a ride through downtown, some neighborhoods, and the business and manufacturing areas. After dinner I keep riding well into the night. I've no design or organized plan and turn onto street after street after street. I look more closely than I've ever looked at any other town on any of my rides and now feel more intimate with Fresno than any other city except Visalia and my current neighborhood in the Los Angeles area. I get back to my room around midnight and described Fresno with these three paragraphs.

THE 99, THE 41, THE 180, THE 168; BLACKSTONE, MCKINLEY, SHAW AND CEDAR. SHADED NEIGHBORHOOD PARKS, LITTER- AND GRAFFITI-FREE STREETS, ROBUST FLORA FRAMING EVERY VIEW. STREETLIGHT BANNERS CLAIMING BIRTH TO WILLIAM SAROYAN. IT'S ABOUT THE CLEAN AND THE NEWLY FABRICATED: REPLICATED CHAIN RESTAURANTS ON EVERY OTHER STREET CORNER, PIZZA PARLORS AND MOVIE COMPLEXES ENCASED IN RED AND PURPLE AND AQUA NEON LIGHTS, GAS STATION MINI MARKETS WITH ARCHED DOORWAYS OF FAUX MASONRY. THE NATURAL CIVIC PRIDE.

TOO, THERE ARE THE HIDDEN PLACES: THE LITTERED AND GRIMED STREETS, A CROOKED HOUSE WITH A MISFITTING FRONT DOOR PAINTED BRIGHT BLUE, THE STUCK-IN-TIME FACTORIES FRONTED BY CRACKED AND BUBBLING ASPHALT, THE CONSTANT PRESS OF STALE, HOT AIR; A FAMILY SPREAD OUT ON EVERY CORNER OF AN INTERSECTION ASKING

FOR DONATIONS FOR THE FUNERAL OF MARIA PORTILLO. BOARDED UP IS A NAMELESS BURGER JOINT THAT CLAIMED ITSELF AS THE ORIGINAL HOME OF THE TEXAS QUARTER POUNDER. A BILLBOARD WITH A MESSAGE FROM GOD THAT SAYS, "WE NEED TO TALK."

IT'S A MICROCOSMED BIG CITY, PUT ASIDE AND IGNORED. IT'S ONE OF THOSE PLACES YOU PASS THROUGH, WE ALL PASS THROUGH, AND BARELY NOTICE. YOU PASS THROUGH BUT THEN STOP AND TURN AROUND AND LOOK. THAT'S WHAT FRESNO DOES, IT MAKES YOU LOOK. IT MAKES YOU LOOK BECAUSE IN THERE, SOMEHOW YOU KNOW IT, AMID THE SPEWED PHLEGM OF METH-HEADS AND WHORES, STRIATED IN THE IMPLORING EYES OF BROKEN VETERANS AND IN THE POETRIES OF RAPPERS SELLING THEIR CDs IN FRONT OF GROCERY STORES; IN THERE BEHIND THE PERFECTLY TRIMMED PALMS AND PINES OF PRECISELY ANGLED APART-MENT COMPLEXES WITH TROPICAL NAMES, INSIDE THE COMPACT BLOCKS OF HYGIENIC, MULTI-STORIED BUSINESS BUILDINGS, IN THE VERY SOULS OF INNUMERABLE LOVING FAMILIES WALKING AND TALKING TOGETHER; IN THERE LIES A SPRAWLING LATTICEWORK, A SILENT RUSH OF GENIUS IGNORED, INSPIRATION MARGINALIZED, FUTURES DISMISSED. LIVES CHOKED. AND YOU WONDER IF THAT, TOO, IS YOU.

The next day, Friday, I head northeast up to Shaver Lake via Auberry Road through the low-lying, grass covered hills and, by pure happenstance, come across Sheri's Roadhouse, an archetypal biker joint: friendly, laid back and an easy conversation no matter where you sit. I have a couple of lemonades and a couple of nice chats with some other patrons while we sit on the back patio watching the squirrels. However, by far the most appealing aspect of the place is the blond behind the bar – I assume it's Sheri – who is a fine, fine looking woman with a magnetic smile, a matching personality, and a contour that inspires my imagination, especially when she runs after the squirrels to chase them out of the place. Thinking about this, I walk back inside and order a third lemonade. Sheri treats me to a few, short and pleasant conversations but she's busy and getting busier, so it's time to head on out.

I pay for my lemonades, take one last, wishful look at Sheri, then get back on Auberry Road, which mostly wig-wags gently through an agreeable countryside. I pass by the bucolic towns of Auberry, Meadow Lakes and Alder Springs and eventually merge with Highway 168, a wide and well-maintained road with an expansive view of the middle of the San Joaquin Valley. Soon I'm riding through the archetypal mountain community of Shaver Lake and right after that is the lake itself. It's a healthy area full of trees and fresh air and families enjoying the gentle waters. After taking a fair amount of photos, I travel back down the 168 with the idea of more lemonade and a future-leaning conversation with Sheri. However, I get lost – none of the people I ask knows where Sheri's Roadhouse is – and end up tired and hungry on Highway 180, south of Fresno and north of Sanger. At least I know where Fresno is so that's where I go, eat dinner, then head back to my motel room where I file my memories of Sheri under the heading of Lost Opportunities.

On Saturday, I take Highway 41 up to Yosemite. Though I'd been there several times as a kid, I have no specific recollections, so this feels like my first visit. Yosemite is one of the most famous national parks and for two good reasons: its glorious beauty and all those incomparable black and white photographs by Ansel Adams. I pull up to the entrance and the park ranger, a pretty and robust woman, tells me that today motorcycles get free admittance. I remark what an excellent policy that is, thank her, then ride the ten or so enjoyable miles to Wawona where I buy some bottled water and beef jerky.

As I'm walking back to my bike, I see the Wawona Golf Course on the other side of the 41. I stop. What, I ask myself, is a golf course doing in the middle of a national park? Now this may sound odd but I generally find golf courses aesthetic – most are perfectly manicured and cleverly laid out – and I always enjoyed the game when I played it in the past. But why, why, why put one in Yosemite, that bounty of nature's best? To my eyes, something so obviously man-made *does not* belong amid Mother Nature's bosom.

I continue along the 41, or Wawona Road as it's now called. It's summertime, meaning it's tourist season, meaning it's as crowded and slow as the Los Angeles Dodgers parking lot after a home game. If it weren't for all the cars, this would be one of the most enjoyable roads I've ever been on.

Normally, when you're in a mountainous area like this, you'd assume you were at a high altitude – it certainly has that feel to it – but this area is only thirty-five hundred feet. It's interesting to compare these lush mountains with the forever flat and treeless scrublands of New Mexico and the drylands of Nevada, which are at twice the elevation. (Not that all of Yosemite is at this elevation; there are places that get up to thirteen thousand feet.)

After twenty or so miles, Wawona Road turns right and becomes Southside Drive, and it's here that I occasionally catch a glimpse of the world famous Half Dome. I'm in the heart of Yosemite Valley, through which runs the sparkling Merced River. I park on the side of the road and walk down to it, and it's the only place in Yosemite I don't see any other people. It's so perfectly unaffected and beautiful that I stand for the longest time quietly saying "Wow" over and over.

At the end of Southside Drive, where there are numerous camp-grounds, cabins for rent, the Yosemite Village, and the Ansel Adams Gallery, the road loops back and I'm on Northside Drive. As the traffic nudges along, I realize that my upset with the Wawona Golf Course is inconsistent. I mean, here I am riding a man-made vehicle on a man-made road with man-made beef jerky in my pocket thinking that some day I'd like to rent a man-made cabin and take a tour of the man-made Ansel Adams Gallery. Why would I be upset over a golf course in nature's bosom but not upset over those other man-made things? It doesn't make sense. So I invent a new word that's the opposite of upset: downset. I'm now downset with the Wawona Golf Course, no longer have an aversion to it, and I'm glad it is where it is.

Despite the slow traffic and having to stop for tourists standing in the middle of the road taking photos, I'm enjoying the sights. It's here, on Northside Drive, that I get closest to El Capitan, a three thousand foot high granite rock with a vertical face. It's a dizzying, unforgettable sight. Despite our paved roads, motorcycles, automobiles, buses, campgrounds, flushing toilets, and golf courses, he looks upon us, unimpressed, with a calm majesty.

I turn left and ride over the short Pohono Bridge, which is neatly lined with cemented rock and crosses the Merced River. It's an ideal place for photos so I immediately pull into a sandy turnout where a woman, carrying nothing but a large purse, is hitchhiking. A hitchhiker in Yosemite is an odd sight so I ask, "Are you actually hitchhiking in Yosemite?" She nods. I raise my eyebrows and nod as well. I go back to the bridge, take my photos and wonder how anyone would come to be hitchhiking here. Yosemite is a place you visit, not pass through to get from one place to another. How did she end up without transportation?

I go back to my bike and call over to her, "Where're you headed?" She shrugs. I nod to the empty seat behind me and say, "Well...." As she walks over I take a close look. She's about thirty years old, slender, has the face of a supermodel, is dressed in an uptown-slutty way and walks like she knows it and doesn't care who else does. She takes my helmet, puts it on, climbs on the back, wraps her arms around my waist and snuggles her bountiful twins into the middle of my back. We take off and I'm thinking this is every man's dream, right?

It's a couple of miles later, right after we get onto Wawona Road, when I begin to get mental flashes of riding over the edge of the road and down the cliffside. Soon, these mental videos become so constant that I barely notice the road. Despite the cool mountain air, I'm sweating bullets the size of bazooka rounds and riding like it's the first time I've been on a motorcycle. I'm actually thankful for the slow moving traffic. No matter what I do, the intensity of these bloody videos keeps growing and growing. I never get visions like that so the only explanation is that they're coming from her, right? Who, exactly, *is* sitting behind me, I wonder. It continues to get worse and worse so that by the time we're half way to Wawona, I'm certain that the uptown-slutty-blond supermodel is actually a three hundred foot tall disfigured ogre hell-bent on laughing at my demise.

When we finally arrive in Wawona, I'm shaking like I've stood in front of a firing squad, eyes wide open, and they all missed by less than a foot. She climbs off, I climb off and I'm greeted with a venomous barrage directed at her "fucking mother", her "fucking kids", and her "fucking husband". I swear her bulging eyes are a sickening yellow, her tongue is forked, and her saliva is blood red. I'm face to face with the devil.

Then, in but a moment, she turns back into the uptown-slutty-blond supermodel and asks, with a tempting smile, how far it is to my room. Despite the bountiful twins pressing against my chest, all of my attention is on two other things: a three hundred foot tall ogre and the miracle that I'm still alive. So I tell her it's only an hour away but I'm sorry I can't take her there because of the helmet law in California; we're sure to get stopped and ticketed and not be allowed to ride any farther. (Can you believe it? A helmet law comes to my rescue!) "Fuck!" explodes out of her mouth and she strides away. Anxious to get away myself – I don't want to hang around and push my luck – I get on my bike and start it up. I look around. It hasn't been five seconds but she's gone. I look all around again and, sure enough, the devil has vanished.

I'm still rattled and feeling hunted when I take off and figure I could use some kind of sanctuary. Not a quarter of a mile later, I see a guy standing next to a brand new Harley Electra Glide in the parking area of an abandoned gas station. He's wearing a dark blue t-shirt on the front of which, in tall, white letters, it says "Bill." Not "I'm Bill" or "My name is Bill" or "This t-shirt belongs to Bill"; it says just "Bill." And there he stands, a sanctuary of unassuming friendliness. I'm lured by the innocent simplicity.

It turns out that Bill is from England. Not long after finishing school, he and his wife unexpectedly ran into a lot of money when the telecommunications firm they helped start up was sold. Since then, they've raised four kids, who are all doing quite well, thank you very much, and have ridden over much of the planet: Great Britain, Scandinavia, Germany, France, Italy, Greece, North Africa, Australia, New Zealand, Canada and the United States. He tells me they've logged over six hundred thousand miles. They're now on their twelfth Harley, which they bought in Montreal and rode west across the United States to an abandoned gas station parking lot in Yosemite where his song-writing wife (forget her name) got on a tour bus and he's now talking with yours truly, a native Californian.

So Bill from England, a rider of the world, is the sanctuary I was looking for. I'm no longer shaking or sweating or mentally watching myself fly over a cliff to certain death. I think about world riders like Bill and his wife and make a wild guess that there are maybe two thousand of them. I've met several and at one point they all say the same thing: far and away, the friendliest people in the world are Americans. When Bill says it, I thank him and feel proud to be a part of that. After an hour or so, the sunlight begins to wane and it's time for me to head back, alone, to my motel. Bill and I shake paws and I tell him he has no idea how happy I am to have met him.

Early the following morning, a Sunday, I get a phone call. The one-week postponement has been shortened to four days so it's time to head back home. I abstain from breakfast and embark on another tour of Fresno. Around 10 A.M., I get on the 99 and head south. Looking left and right, I see the verdant farmland I remember as a kid. However, I can't help thinking about the vast area farther west that's known as the San Joaquin Valley Dust Bowl.

You may think the root cause is a lack of water – it's happened before – but it's not. The real cause is the government, Federal and State, via the Environmental Protection Agency. Together, they decided that several fish species needed to be protected from irrigation water and irrigation pumps, which they believe may cause them to become extinct. The plan they came up with was to divert irrigation water away from the farms and to the Sacramento Delta and the San Francisco Bay. In other words, a drought has been created by regulations.

What was once one of the great breadbaskets of the world is now an unkempt and litter-filled centerpiece of want, waste and fifteen to forty percent unemployment that covers over a half-million acres. I won't mention the paradox of a government agency that's supposed to protect our environment causing all that litter and waste. A paradox I *will* mention is that despite their efforts, the numbers of these endangered fish continues to dwindle and the environment is in a higher state of uncertainty than it was before. The worst of it, however, are the tens of thousands of people who are now unemployed and forced to live off the government dole, something that costs California taxpayers sixty to 120 million dollars a month.

Some environmentalists claim that other problems have arisen *because of* irrigation water. I've no doubt that some of those claims are true but to what degree they're true, I don't know. But I do know one thing: Whether you believe the San Joaquin Valley deserves the irrigation water or not, there is one inarguable fact: the EPA's efforts to protect or save the environment in the San Joaquin Valley have not worked, either for the fish, for the environment, or for the people who live here.

Okay, rant over.

I continue south past Fowler, Selma, the Swedish community of Kingsburg, and over the Kings River, which is dotted with houseboats. When I pass the 198 Freeway, I give a nod to my Visalia and wish it well. Thirty-five minutes later, I pull off at the Avenue 16 exit in order to gas up and eat at the Akal Travel Plaza. One thing I always wonder about this place is how it's pronounced: AY-kul, ay-KAL, AH-kul or ah-KAL? I also always plan to ask someone but I never remember to do so.

As I pull into the gas station, the most obvious thing in view is an enormous old, brown motorhome that's so long it's taking up the space beside four pumps. Bent over the steering wheel is an exhausted old man staring straight ahead. The sliding door is open and inside are three or four kids quietly playing. I get my gas then go inside the Plaza, which is a convenience store on one side and an array of miniature fast food places on the other.

I spend a good while deciding what to eat and eventually order chicken and fries, then promise myself that someday I'll eat a vegetable. Maybe even a green one. Walking around the place is a thickset woman wearing modestly priced jewelry and clothes that are worn but neat and clean. She's earnestly asking for money from each patron. All she needs is enough for gas so she and her family can make it home to Bakersfield. And maybe a little for food for her hungry kids. Despite being in a desperate situation she is polite and I like her for that. I figure that all she needs is twenty dollars but no one is coming forth with any coin. I also expect she'll soon approach me but she never does. It's understandable. I need a shave and a shower (and probably smell like it), my hair is long and wind-battered, and I'm giving the impression that I haven't been a member of a civilized society for months.

But that's understandable as well. The more you ride, the more spartan your wardrobe becomes. You end up wearing and packing only the things that are immediately functional and because you're riding in the open air, your few clothes quickly become dirty and tattered.

While waiting for my lunch, I remember my first few multi-day rides and how I would pack nice shoes in case I would, you know, end up going to a nice place. Well, if I'm going to wear nice shoes, I'll need a nice shirt and a nice pair of pants. A nice jacket, too. The problem is, these things take up room. Too much room. On one of those early trips, I bought some souvenirs but they wouldn't fit anywhere because everything on the bike was already tightly packed. I had to ride with one bag between my legs while holding the other bag with my teeth. Of course I couldn't continue riding thousands of miles like this (the dental bill would have been astronomical) so I found a post office and got a box. First went in the nice shoes, then the pants, the jacket, the shirt, and finally the souvenirs. I mailed it home and that was the last time I packed anything that wasn't immediately functional.

My reverie is broken by the kid behind the counter.

Kid Behind the Counter: Excuse me, sir, are you forty-seven?

Me: *(Perplexed)* I'm sorry, am I what?

Kid Behind the Counter: Forty-seven. Are you forty-seven?

Me: *(Finally realizing he must mean my order number, I look at my receipt)* Ah! Yes! I'm forty-seven! How'd you know?

I take my food outside and sit two tables away from the entrance, next to which three, male local yokels in their twenties are standing.

The earnest and polite woman goes out to the motorhome and says something to her father and kids, then walks back to find her twenty-dollar patron. She asks the local yokels for money each time she passes and each time they decline to help. After she goes inside, they take turns mocking her and laugh hysterically. They look my way every now and again hoping for at least a chuckle of approval, but instead I just stare. As the minutes pass, my empathy for the woman grows. I want to help but she's still avoiding me so I follow her with my eyes, waiting for her to look my way. She goes to the local yokels for a third time, pleading for something, anything. They say something mean and petty about having jobs and if she had one she wouldn't need to panhandle from strangers. That's when I change my mind about the twenty dollars.

Finally, she looks my way. I curl my finger to motion her over and she slowly walks the twenty feet to my table. Without saying a word, I reach into my pocket and hand her forty dollars. She stands, frozen and shocked. Tears form. She gently takes the money, profusely thanks me then runs over to the motorhome, says something to her father and kids, then runs into the market while shouting what a wonderful man I am. A few minutes later, the father is pumping gas and she walks out with both arms full of soda and candy for the kids.

The local yokels are chagrined. One of them shouts to me that she didn't spend all the money, hoping I'll demand my change and embarrass her further. I tell him it doesn't matter, it's her money now, not mine. This shuts them up for good and they leave. Right before the family takes off, the woman jumps out of the motorhome and runs over. With eyes wide and wet she earnestly grasps my hand and says: You are blessed in the afterlife, *you* are *blessed* in the afterlife.

The family leaves and I take off a few minutes afterward. When I get back on the 99, I think about how much more full my life is because of the people I have met on this trip. From the waitress giving me free pie, to Sheri and her charms, to Bill, the sanctuary of friendliness, to the earnest and polite woman who blessed my afterlife. Someday, I'm certain, even the three local yokels will grow up and become charitable. But what of the devil in Yosemite? Well, maybe she's only there to show us that the dark makes the light more bright.

Up ahead, slowly making its way to Bakersfield, is the motorhome. Inside are children who know their mother loves them and will always get them home safely, and a father who is proud of the good woman his little girl has grown up to be. For a time I think of my own family and smile. Just before Bakersfield I pass by the motorhome and honk. The father honks back and they all wave and smile. As the other freeway travelers and I pass each other, I glance at their profiles and marvel at the gratifying riches to be had just by living on our sublime earth.

The motorhome gradually disappears in my rearview mirror and when I get to the other side of Bakersfield, it is gone. I am alone with the 99, the backbone of the San Joaquin Valley, the birthplace of my heart. I think about that hardwearing, asphalt nobleman, as it is and as it was, and I fear that until now I have missed his lesson. All those times I traveled it, I had been looking for beauty and bounty, for excitement and adventure, for inspiration; I had wanted those things to be visible, to be presented to me when, truly, they have always existed within.

I'll soon merge with the I-5, which I can now see to my right; farther ahead is the Grapevine wiggling its way into the mountains. I look in my rearview mirror once again and see the 99, my foundation, stretching forever behind me.

5

GODDESSES and a PORK CHOP

There are many things you can control when riding: speed, lean angle, lane position, stuff like that. But there are many more things you can't control, like the weather and road conditions. The reason you can't control those things is because they're actually under the charge of the Goddesses of Riding. Now, you might think that, maybe, you could at least influence these goddesses in some way to make your ride more pleasant, but it's not possible. I know. I've tried. Over and over. It's a lost cause. The reason it's a lost cause, for me at least, is because they're goddesses, which means they're women, which means I'm clueless as to what to do.

I don't know how many Goddesses of Riding there are but I do know that they each fall into one of two categories: Good and Evil. It's like that good witch/bad witch thing from The Wizard of Oz. In the good category are, among others, the Perfect-Road-Surface Goddess, the No-Cars-on-the-Road Goddess, and the Gorgeous-Scenery Goddess. We all like the good goddesses. They're sweet and protective and like bikers.

Then there are the evil goddesses, all of whom have been thoroughly trained by Misery, their matriarch patron saint. Most evil goddesses, like the Chuckhole Goddess, the Stuck-Next-to-Someone-Who's-Texting Goddess, and the Bugs-Bigger-than-the-Statue-of-Liberty Goddess, come and go according to their own whim. (By the bye, have you ever noticed that when someone is texting, they slow down and veer to the left?) However, there are three evil goddesses who show up more often than the rest and thereby cause more problems than the rest. They are, of course, Wind, Rain, and the two-faced goddess Hot-n-Cold. For some reason, they don't like me these days.

It's Autumn in the Pacific Northwest. I'm trying to mind my own business while riding east out of Boise, Idaho on Interstate 84, but the goddesses Wind and Cold are right there, torturously pounding me all the way. (Lurking somewhere, ready to pounce, is Rain, I know it.) This is not relaxing. Or safe. All I can think about is making it to Pocatello with my wits and bones intact. Add to it all the road construction (another evil goddess) and it seems I won't get there till next spring. I stop for a snack and to get warm at a convenience store in Jerome and as I walk out with my beef jerky and hot chocolate, a group of guys in their late twenties wearing full camo outfits (it's hunting season) walk in. A few minutes later, they walk out, joking and laughing and bantering about.

So I'm sitting there listening to their conversation, which isn't really a conversation because a guy named Jake is doing all the talking, and all he's talking about are women. Loudly. My first impression is that at the age of say, twenty-eight, he finally managed to lose his virginity last night, but I'm quickly proven wrong when he says he knows everything about women. This is amazing to me because here he is, not yet thirty years old, and he knows everything about women while I've been working on that my whole life and know nothing about them. One by one, his friends walk away (wonder why?) and he ends up talking to only me. Of course, I'm honored and hang on to every word because I want to know everything about women. (Also, I hope, if I can learn his secrets about women, maybe I'll finally be able to exert some persuasion over the Evil Goddesses of Riding!) Gentlemen, pay heed; this is the wisdom we have always yearned for.

Jake, the Woman Whisperer: Y'see, all that candy 'n' flower shit don't mean shit.

Me: *(Staring, mouth open in wonder)*

Jake, the Woman Whisperer: Alls they want is a guy that has shit 'n' *is* the shit.

Me: *(Nodding)*

Jake, the Woman Whisperer: There ain't any other shit than that shit. Know what I mean?

Me: Yep, that's the shit.

He then strides like *a man* to his rusted, beat up, dirt covered Jeep, carrying a 12-pack of Bud Light and a box of Rough Rider condoms. I am in awe. When he is done, the world of women finally will have been conquered.

I continue riding east but I'm still so in awe over Jake's vast wisdom that I don't notice much about the environment. Except for the goddesses Wind and Cold. For some reason they still have me in their crosshairs and I can't get them to go away, or at least be a little kind. The problem I'm having is that I can't figure out how to apply Jake's techniques to them. It's my fault, though. I should have listened more closely. In my motel room in Pocatello, I check the weather forecast and tomorrow Wind and Cold will be even more riled up. And there's a forty percent chance Rain will come and visit. So I decide to stay an extra day in my warm and dry motel room and, you know, be warm and dry.

The next day I'm all warm and dry but figure I'll have another go at appeasing the evil goddesses. I decide to backtrack thirty-five miles to the Massacre Rocks State Park, where I want to get some photos of incredible rock formations along the Snake River. Bad idea. Cold has decided it will be in the mid-forties, Wind can't make up her mind which way to come at me, and Rain decides to show up as soon as I get on the freeway. The freeway where there are trucks. Big trucks. Double- and triple-trailer trucks.

Now, I'm going a little slower than the speed limit but those double- and triple-trailer trucks aren't. They don't have to. Those drivers are completely sheltered from the evil goddesses and don't have to worry about them as much as I do. In fact, their cabs are so big and luxurious that they probably have hot tubs, masseuses, and flat screen TVs, so they're not even aware of how abusive these evil goddesses are. To make matters worse, Wind decides to play an evil practical joke. Right when a big truck in the fast lane is passing me, she blows my bike three feet toward him. That's when I do something smart (imagine!) and get off at the next exit and go back to my warm and dry motel room where I'll be, you know, warm and dry.

It's a little colder the next day (low forties) but at least it's not raining, so I head north on Interstate 15. I do something smart again (what?) and buy some long johns and a second thermal undershirt at the Walmart in Idaho Falls. Now that I'll be warmer, I decide to ride up Highways

33 and 28 to Salmon, which the Walmart cashier claims is a beautiful mountain area.

I'm disappointed. The 160 miles to Salmon go through nondescript, grass-covered hills with low mountains to the east and west, so there aren't even any interesting sights to take my mind off the numbing cold.

But the real issue is that my extra layers of clothing must have angered the goddess Cold, or challenged her in some way, because once I get past Mud Lake, she drops the temperature into the mid-thirties and I still have 120 miles to go. It's brutal. Despite all my layers of clothing I'm shivering so hard I can't keep the handlebars still and my clattering teeth are louder than my engine.

I've just about turned into a total body-shaking, teeth-clattering zombie when an odd thought pops into my mind about this pork chop that's way back in the bottom corner of my freezer at home. I get the idea that he's angry with me for ignoring him for over a year, and that he's somehow gotten into a cabal with the Evil Goddesses of Riding, and they've decided to transform me, yours truly, into a frozen pork chop so I'll know what it's like. You know, poetic justice and all that.

Anyway, pork chop or not, I'm faced with making a choice. If I slow down, I'll be less cold but colder longer; if I speed up, I'll be more cold but get to Salmon faster. What to do, what to do, what to do.... One choice is better than the other, I'm sure, but because all twelve of my functioning brain cells are frozen solid, I can't even remember what those two choices are.

This area south of Salmon must be great for hunting because all the men (except yours truly) are wearing camo and have big pickups and big rifles. And most are carrying a sidearm. One guy I meet, Vard ("like in boulevard"), tells me that he and his three sons bagged three elk that morning. Each son is taking one home so he has to go out tomorrow morning and get one for himself. It's odd but fascinating to me because this is a brand of testosterone that you just don't see in the Los Angeles metropolitan area where I live.

The next day, I head north through the Bitterroot National Forest and unlike the area south of Salmon, it's real pretty. US Highway 93 follows the Salmon River, the mountains are closer, the vegetation and trees are more colorful, and the river must be good for fishing because there are fly fishermen all along. And it's warmed up a bit. In fact, it's way up in the mid-forties. After what I went through yesterday, it's so warm I think I could ride in shorts, a tank top, and flip-flops. (Uhhh, no.) Even the goddess Wind is taking a breather. And Rain? Well, she's probably crying a river somewhere else.

When the 93 slips into Montana, it goes up into higher mountains. Evidently, those twelve functioning brain cells aren't functioning too well because, again, I've decided on a route that's not too smart. It's really cold now. And I mean *really* cold. So cold that I can barely turn my head and when I do manage to turn my head I see snow next to the road. It's so cold that it feels like I've been condemned to a frozen hell by an angry pork chop. On the other hand, it's grandly beautiful, the kind of place where views become vistas, and in that sense I'm glad to be here.

I make it to Missoula, get a motel room and congratulate myself on not getting frostbite, but it takes most of the night for my twelve semi-functioning brain cells to thaw out.

The following day I head west on Interstate 90 and the three Evil Goddesses are full-bore in a hellacious catfight. It's crazy. Swirling, waterlogged and brain cells freezing crazy. My body quickly gets to the point where it's essentially useless, so I tell The Beast that it's up to him to get us safely through the 160 miles to Coeur d'Alene. And he does, just like he always has and always will.

The I-90 from Missoula to Coeur D'Alene is breathtaking. The first half goes through the Lolo National Forest and the second half is in Idaho's Panhandle. It's mountainous but the altitude never gets over five thousand feet. By the time the Rockies have gotten this far north, they've sobered up and settled down from their high altitude intoxication in Colorado. But they're still the Rockies: angular, grand and spirit-filled.

I cross over the Clark Fork River a number of times and take a few side roads. I find intimate places, unique places, and I get the feeling that I'm the only one who's ever seen them. There's a dirt road that weaves through winding rock walls on the right and towering forest on the left, and it is magic. I stand on an old wooden bridge that's no longer fit for vehicle traffic. I can see and hear the purling waters below me, and for a time I look at the way the mist cuddles its way through the Pines and golden-turning Aspens, the way the sun back-lights the clouds, the way the river is unaffected by all around her.

I make it to Coeur d'Alene (pronounced cor-da-LANE by the local folks) and what an ideal place to end my ride for the day! It's clean, orderly and upscale, and sits on the shores of the Coeur d'Alene Lake, which fans out forever like an exploding sapphire. The sky is a lighter blue than the waters, the white and gray clouds are weightless, and the trees and mountains echo birdsongs heard nowhere else. If you take the Scenic Byway off the I-90, you'll ride more than sixty miles on one of the most enjoyable roads ever designed, and all the while the lake is right there at your side, the mountainside on the other. But it really doesn't matter where you go or what you do, or even if you just sit and breathe. The air glitters.

My trip through Washington begins with a new rear tire at the Lone Wolf Harley dealership in Spokane, where I immediately find out that Spokane is pronounced spo-KAN, not spo-KAYN. Afterward, I notice that the state highway signs have a silhouette of George Washington on them and wonder if the state was actually named after the good president. (Turns out that it was.) Then a kid working at a convenience store tells me that Washington is the only state in the United States with rain forests. Isn't that something! The things you learn on the road.

I head west on US Highway 2 into scattered showers and temperatures in the mid-forties, and for the sixth day in a row, I am to-the-bone cold. For the first ninety miles, there's really nothing to take my mind off my cold bones because the views are pretty much unremarkable. Until I ride over the Dry Falls Dam. Right there, amid all that unremarkable-ness, Dry Falls Lake seems to stretch out for countless miles, the islands in it like distant, uncharted lands, strange and forbidding. The reflection of the clouds in the fluted, glassy surface is like a giant watercolor painting that slowly moves, the reflection of the sky being several shades darker than the sky itself. The surface is not far below the level of the road and it is as if I'm gliding across enchanted waters.

Right after the dam, I head southwest on Highway 17 and immediately see a sign for the Dry Falls Interpretive Area. I can't recall ever seeing an "Interpretive Area" and don't know what that would be, but figure I'll go check it out. I still don't know what the area is interpreting or who might be interpreting the area but I do know that Dry Falls is one primeval place with still lakes and uncivilized islands looking up at the vertical, serrated cliffs.

On the informative signs, I read some fantastic facts that are hard to fathom. During the last ice age, about ten thousand years ago, the largest waterfall in the history of the world was right here. It was four miles wide and eight hundred feet high until the waters eroded it down to "only" four hundred feet. The river that ran over it was three hundred feet deep, moved along at sixty-five miles-per-hour, spewed several *cubic miles* of rock, and carried *ten times* more water than all the current rivers of the world combined.

After Dry Falls, Highway 17 follows, in succession, the shores of Park Lake, Blue Lake, Alkali Lake, Lenore Lake (the largest) and finally Soap Lake. Here and there, across icy blue waters, are houses and recreation areas in the forested hillsides. After that, the landscape goes back to being farmland, but soon I catch sight of the serpentine shaped Moses Lake to the right. The area surrounding it is wooded and lush, and it strikes me as an ideal place to live if you like taking nature photos. When the 17 meets Interstate 90, it's late afternoon and the temperature is dropping so I decide to spend the night on the west side of Moses Lake.

One other big problem I'm having this trip is money, lack of. And wouldn't you know it, this has become the ride of high expenses. Everything costs more than I'd expected, plus I hadn't anticipated that new tire in Spokane. Now, I know I should buy a heated vest and heated gloves—should have bought them a week ago—but if I do that, I may not have enough for food, gas and lodging to get home. And if I did make it home, what would I do about the bills piling up on my desk? I'm spending money on this ride, not making it. So I have to make do with what I have.

The following morning, I look at the map and figure that, despite the ominous presence of Misery's three Evil Goddesses, I can make it to Hood River, which is only 230 miles away. I layer on as many clothes as I can layer on but there are serious deficiencies. Like a half helmet with no ear flaps or face guard, holes in both pairs of socks, no heated vest, no heated gloves, no glove liners. Then there's the wool sleeve that covers my face and blocks the wind with the efficiency of a chain link fence.

Nevertheless, I confidently head east on the I-90 but during the first stretch, the cold rain (it's in the low forties) is so thick and hard that I have to pull over after only twenty-six miles. I warm up a bit at a gas station but afterward, the cold wind and rain (it's in the thirties now) force me to pull over at every place it's possible to pull over. Eight miles, four miles, six miles, it doesn't matter. Right after the marvelous Vantage Bridge, I walk around for a while to take photos and warm up a bit. (Believe me, walking in mid-thirties temperature is much warmer than riding in it.) As soon as I get back on the bike, however, I'm freezing again.

The constant torment of Misery and her three Evil Goddesses convinces me to forget about making it to Hood River, so I start thinking about Yakima, which is only seventy miles away. Then there's Ellensburg, which is only thirty miles away. Actually, at this point I don't care where I end up as long as there's a warm motel room and a hot shower. The problem is the thirty miles from here to Ellensburg, which consists of nothing but constant rain, mid-thirties temperature, high winds and no amenities. I start to think about the wisdom of doing what I'm doing but there's nothing to think about because there *is no* wisdom in what I'm doing. But even if there was some wisdom, I wouldn't be able to think about it because my head is being frozen by a vindictive pork chop. I'm in a daze when I get back on the freeway and five miles later, it begins to snow.

Snow. Snow? Did I say Snow? YES! SNOW!!! So here it is, 32 degrees *at the most* and I'm dressed like a beachcomber in the Bahamas. There are no turnoffs, the big trucks are splashing me with gallons of freezing water, the wind is howling, and my chances for survival are lowering faster than my body heat.

The pork chop has won. I now know what it feels like to sit, neglected, in a freezer for over a year. I'm on the verge of shuffling off my mortal coil and wonder if that movie-of-my-life will flash before my eyes, but my brain is so frozen, I figure all I'll get is an out-of-focus snapshot or two.

My brain starts to short circuit and odd memories keep popping up, like a poem I memorized when I was twelve years old by Robert William Service. It's called the "The Cremation of Sam McGee" and it tells the story of Sam, who had spent most of his life hunting for gold in the forever frozen Yukon. He comes to hate the cold so much that he makes his friend promise to cremate him after he dies so his passing-on will be warm. Sam does pass on and the friend dutifully follows through with his promise because "… a promise made is a debt unpaid, and the trail has its own stern code …." At the end of the poem, Sam is sitting in the middle of this huge bonfire with a big smile on his face. He says, "Since I left Plumtree, down in Tennessee, it's the first time I've been warm." For the first time in my life, I can fully commiserate with ol' Sam.

After an eternity of thirteen miles, I peer through the snow flurries just in time to see the turnoff for the Ryegrass Safety Rest Area. Hallelujah! I head straight to the bathroom and, mercy of mercies, there are two (count 'em, 2) hot air hand dryers. Can I get an Amen! I stay in that bathroom for well over an hour, warming my hands and trying to dry my gloves and everything else.

As I thaw out and begin to get thoughts again, the first thought that I get is how absurd, even comical, all this is. I mean, what the hell am I doing? Every guy who walks in must think it's absurd as well because they each stop and stare a few seconds like, well, like anyone would stare at a frozen pork chop under a hot air hand dryer. The comments begin after they've washed their hands.

Bathroom Patron #1: Damn cold fer ridin'!

Me: Got that right.

Bathroom Patron #2: Ain't it too cold fer a motorcycle?

Me: Yes!

Bathroom Patron #3: You're actually riding a motorcycle in the snow?

Me: Yes.

Bathroom Patron #4: Dangerous riding in the snow, ain't it?

Me: Yes!

Bathroom Patron #5: Think it's a good idea to be ridin' in the snow?

Me: No.

Bathroom Patron #6: What the hell are you doing ridin' in the snow?

45

Me: Freezing.
Bathroom Patron #7: Cold?
Me: Yes!
Bathroom Patron #8: Hot enough for ya?
Me: Hah!
Bathroom Patron #9: Warmed up yet?
Me: No.
Bathroom Patron #10: *(Shakes his head in disbelief.)*
Me: *(Nods in agreement.)*

Seventeen miles. That's what's between me and that hot shower in a warm motel room in Ellensburg, and an escape from death. I have to do it. I mean, I can't spend all night in a public bathroom, though I'm seriously considering it. I get as warm as I can get, run out to my snow-covered bike, jump on and take off. It's not going well. All that warmth dissipates in a minute and I'm back to being a frozen pork chop. In desperation, I cry out to that lonely guy in my freezer: I know how you feel! I'm sorry! Please forgive me! It'll never happen again!

My plea for forgiveness must have made an impression because five miles before Ellensburg, I'm blessed with a small deliverance when the snow turns into rain. Yes! The temperature is no longer below freezing! For the first time in over six hours my chances for survival are going up. I arrive in Ellensburg, get that warm room, take a hot shower, and I'm no longer a frozen pork chop. But then, I think, it took a full seven hours to go only seventy miles so maybe I am a pork chop after all. But at least now I'm a thawed out pork chop.

The following morning there is no snow, no rain, very little wind, there's more blue sky than clouds and the temperature is "way up" in the mid-forties. Sunbathing weather! That apology really worked!

I've long since learned that a good waitress knows everything there is to know about everything, and if you have good manners, she'll happily tell you everything you want to know about anything. Last night, Sadie the waitress tells me that Highway 821 to Yakima is a lot prettier and more interesting than Interstate 82. So I head off down the 821. What a terrific and fun road! Fun not only because I'm no longer a freezing pork chop but also because of the road itself. It parallels the winding Yakima River, the mountains are within reach, the trees are fluorescent, and the river gleams. It's one of those rides where everything goes perfectly. There's a special thrill when you hit every corner at the exact right spot, the exact right angle and the exact right speed; it's effortless and it seems like you're going a thousand miles and hour. You become weightless.

I pass through Yakima, which is officially known as the Palm Springs of Washington, and at Toppenish, take Highway 97 south. It's a clean, mountainous area that's as gorgeous as the day. At the beginning there's road construction and about fifty of us have to wait for the pilot car. Soon after we take off, there's no more road construction so I pull over to take some photos. When I get back on the road, everyone else is long gone and I have it all to myself. I do not see another vehicle for the entire fifty miles. Fifty miles of blessed and broad sweepers, fifty miles of forest-covered mountains, fifty miles of beaming blue skies and friendly clouds, fifty miles of clean air that crackles with the scent of pine.

Eventually, Highway 97 crosses over the Columbia River, which is the boundary between Washington and Oregon. I'm on the Oregon side going west on Interstate 84 but I never lose sight of Washington to the north. This section of the I-84, from Highway 97 to Portland, is one of the more beautiful interstates anywhere. The road surface is accommodating and the constantly changing shadows from the constantly changing cloudscape make me feel like I'm riding through Mother Nature's kaleidoscope. To my right, the noble Columbia River faithfully follows her chosen path from the Rockies in Canada, through the Pacific Northwest and into the Pacific Ocean.

At sunset, it begins to rain so I spend the night in Troutdale. The following morning, I make it to Interstate 5 and finally head south for good. Yes! South to the promised land of warmth and dry roads!

This stretch of the I-5 is also one of the more picturesque interstates, and Oregon is every bit as beautiful as you've heard it to be. I cross the border into California amid one glorious mountain view after another and just north of Weed come to the fitting end of my autumn trip to the Pacific Northwest.

I reflect on the past two weeks. True, the fact that I hadn't dressed properly for the weather had put me in danger (lesson learned) but other than that, I did do a few things right. There were many times when the conditions were simply hazardous, but because I always stayed fully aware of my surroundings and my own current physical condition, I never compounded those hazards. In other words, I always adjusted my riding to match my "now" skill set.

Perhaps the most important thing, however, was that I kept going. I kept going and got through. When you do that, you realize, as we all have many times, that you can always depend on yourself and your bike, and that is, indeed, a fine feeling.

I'm standing on the shoulder of a side road while the late afternoon sun gently lays a warmth on my back, a promise for the future. I take in the view. There, standing in front of me like long-time lovers holding hands, are the mountains Shasta and Shastina. Low clouds encircle their base making it seem as if they're disconnected from the earth, and their pure white snow against the pure blue sky eliminates all sense of distance and perspective. The round, translucent moon rises behind them, a giant eye of innocence and wonder. Close enough to touch.

6

THE BEST REASON

The best reason to do anything is no reason at all. I first heard that truism when I was a boy and since then I've come across it many times. I've even said it myself, or some variation of it, many times. If you've ever done anything simply for the helluvit, you know what I mean. There's an inexplicable satisfaction associated with it and when you think about it, the only fitting satisfaction with doing something for the helluvit *should be* inexplicable.

I was once in New Mexico waiting to check in to a motel. In front of me, checking in, was an old biker and his lady. They were from Pennsylvania and the clerk remarked that that was a long way to ride on a motorcycle and that their journey would have been a lot more comfortable in a car. He made several other remarks about miles and motorcycles. Just a lonely guy trying to make conversation. The old biker nodded a few times and didn't say much. The clerk finally asked them why they ride so much. The old biker sighed and said, "Oh, we just do." Perfect answer.

Doing something for no reason is what I call a Helluvit. Whenever you want, just go in a direction and wherever you end up is wherever you end up. The freedom of it is undeniable and it's a supreme way to *really* get to know any area. It's a supreme way find out more about yourself as well. Occasionally, when I'm in one of my Helluvits, I try and come up with reasons why I'm doing what I'm doing. Without fail, the effort corrupts the whole activity, drains the fun out of it, and I'm down to a dull level of practicality. Eventually, I quit with the reason-finding and just enjoy the ride. And oftentimes, my Helluvit is just that: a ride.

I'm on one of my few rides where I have a specific destination and a specific time to be there, a situation that always challenges my helluvit skills. In other words, can I make it there on time and still enjoy some Helluvits? The destination is a nice suburb northwest of Denver where Jasmine and Omar and Travis, my younger daughter, son-in-law and grandson live. Travis isn't quite five years old and I'd promised to be there for his cousin Rio's seventh birthday party at Chuck E Cheese.

The trip starts in an exciting way. I'm riding 70 mph going north out of the Los Angeles area on Interstate 5 when, in my rearview mirrors, I see two cars weaving in and out of traffic at over 100 mph. That youthful urge to race, I guess. They're close when one of them pulls into my lane right behind me. I yank The Beast hard to the right and that's when I'm introduced to Mr. Chuckhole. He's nine inches deep, three feet across and sits four miles from the bottom of the Grapevine. Our roadway introduction dents my front rim, jars my rear taillight loose and makes my butt feel like it's been split in two.

The dent in the rim is pretty severe but the front tire is okay and seems to be holding air just fine. I decide I can make it to Visalia, where I'd planned on spending the night anyway, and get the rim fixed the next day. It takes a couple of hours longer than usual but I make it to my friend Kathryn Ann's place in Visalia without another roadway introduction or any loss of air. (I checked every twenty minutes.) The next morning, I start making calls to repair shops, most of which are closed on Mondays. (Why is that?) I finally find a place that's open, Visalia Custom Chrome, and ride on over. Jeff says he can fix the rim but he has no way to pull off the tire.

Visalia Kawasaki is the only motorcycle place open on Mondays so I ride on over there so they can take off the tire, but Jesse and Ryan are swamped with other customers, so I have to wait. Kathryn Ann picks me up, we eat lunch then wait some more. I finally get the rim at 3:25 P.M. and we race back over to Visalia Custom Chrome but run into another problem: the heavy traffic of students getting out of Redwood High School. I swear, getting through this is almost as hard as getting through the candy aisle in a Walmart Superstore a day before Halloween. Nevertheless, we persist and triumph. Jeff fixes the rim quickly and we barely make it back to Visalia Kawasaki before they close. Sometime around 6:30 P.M., the bike is ready to roll.

I take a shower, eat a tasty dinner, pack up, load up and I'm on my way. Yeah, later than I'd planned but, hey, I made it! Thanks to four heroes: Jeff, Jesse, Ryan and Kathryn Ann who cheerfully schlepped around a smelly, sweat-soaked, unshaven biker *and* made him dinner!

I head north on US Highway 99 and arrive at Sally's house in Sacramento around 2 A.M., twelve hours behind schedule. Sally is a good friend and, despite the late hour, she is in such a terrific mood and is such a supreme conversationalist that we stay up till dawn. Most of the next day, too. I finally leave Sally's place around 2 A.M. Thursday morning, which gives me thirty-eight hours to do over 1100 miles. It's nowhere near impossible but it does mean my helluvit inclinations will be challenged even more.

My first stop is Lake Tahoe and I decide to take US Highway 50. The road is in excellent shape but there are stretches that are being worked on. Its path through the forest-laden mountains is stimulating but comfortable, and the miles fly by like a young nighthawk looking for a mate.

It's chilly when I get into the El Dorado National Forest so I pull over to put on a long sleeved t-shirt and my jacket. When I step off the bike, I feel like something hostile is watching me but I try to ignore it and open my bag. Then, for some stupid reason, I begin to think about all those slasher movies I've seen and I begin to imagine that that some*thing* is actually a some*one*. A big, bald and ugly someone with bushy eyebrows, a hatchet and a lust for blood. I peer into the dark bushes for a minute but it's a moonless night so there's nothing to see but a whole lot of darkness.

A branch cracks and I freeze. I'm thinking that when I hop on the bike there'll be a point where my back is turned to the bushes and that's when that someone will trounce. Slowly, I build up my courage, close the bag, get on The Beast and scoot on out of there as fast as I can. I look in my rearview mirror half expecting to see a madman with bushy eyebrows and a hatchet running after me but, of course, there's nothing. I quickly calm down and realize it was probably just a newborn squirrel looking at me and thinking, "Gosh! What's that?"

Not long afterward, I put on my jacket and not long after that I ride over Echo Summit (7,377 feet). It feels like going over the top of the first rise on a big roller coaster and when I descend into the darkness, my heartbeat cranks up a several ticks. Though there's nothing to actually see (it's still nighttime), I sense a disposition of splendor all around. I pass through Lake Tahoe before dawn, my first time in this area on a motorcycle, and I've a small regret that I can't appreciate the sights.

I'm sitting in an all-night diner in Carson City when I decide to continue east on Highway 50 through the Nevada desert. Why I decide on Highway 50 instead of heading up to Interstate 80, I don't know. Interstate 80 isn't much farther north and will probably be a faster route and easier on the ol' derrière. Also, being an interstate freeway, there are bound to be a lot more places to get gas and food, and probably several shady rest areas. I don't know if Interstate 80 in Nevada is actually like that, but it at least seems like a good possibility.

The late summer weather is perfect but that's only because it's nighttime. I know that this will dramatically change for the worse once I find myself in daylight, it being summertime in the desert and all. But right now I don't care about that. All I care about is that I'm riding through a perfectly cool night when there are very few other travelers, fully enjoying my solitary Helluvit.

Basically, Highway 50, also called the Lincoln Highway, goes east and west through the middle of the Nevada desert, and it is a fact that it's the loneliest road in America. I know this because every now and again there are official State of Nevada signs that say it is: HIGHWAY 50, THE LONELIEST ROAD IN AMERICA. (The veracity of this, of course, is made on the dubious assumption that when state officials write something it must be true.) At first I think these signs are just a cute thing for the State of Nevada to spend money on; you know, make the tourists feel like they're on an adventure. Later, as I'm riding under an unrelenting sun and sweating like a sumo wrester running a marathon in the Sahara Desert, I realize that what it *really* is, is a subtle hint that maybe you ought to turn back and find a different route. Like Interstate 80 with its numerous gas stations, air conditioned eateries and shady rest areas.

I ride through the night, pass by Silver Springs, then ride into a pale sunrise right after Fallon, the night escaping in wisps of spectral chill. After passing Highway 722, I make a broad right turn to the other side of an indifferent row of hills and it is here that I have my first close-up look at the Nevada desert. The dry and flat land is without any vibrant vegetation, the color spectrum one of small gradations from ashen yellow to creamy brown. In the distance, the low and lonely mountains are like crumpled, thrown-away slate covered in millennial dust.

Once the sun clears the horizon the temperature rapidly rises. As usual, my mind goes to and fro with odd thoughts and disconnected musings, one of which is that there are stretches of the 50 that are a grand testament to the highway engineer's ability to draw a straight line. Really. If you ever ride this route, there will be times you'll look into the hazy distance at something five miles ahead that *seems* like it might be a bend in the road and you'll get as ecstatic as a cocker spaniel seeing his owner for the first time in a week. Especially if you're sweating as much as that sumo wrestler.

I take a short tour of the next town, Austin. It's mildly hilly and the roads are either pavement, dirt, or a mixture of dirt and rock. On the east side of town is a sign on top of a rise that says the elevation is 7484 feet. I live in Southern California and am somewhat familiar with the Mojave Desert and part of that desert is Death Valley, which is a couple of hundred feet *below* sea level, so to find a desert at over seven thousand feet is surprising. At the rise are a couple of twisties, a welcomed change, so I go back and ride them again. It's a Helluvit thing.

My two-minute twistie ride over, I hunker down, engulfed in sweltering heat, to eat up more miles, but along the way decide to ride up some dirt roads. The roads aren't long and I come across nothing out of the ordinary. When I reach the end of the second one, I realize I'm on private property and figure it'd be a good idea if stayed on public roads.

I'm back on the 50 and it's not long before I notice that all of my thoughts have to do with the nature-made oven I'm riding through. It's a logical thing to think about, considering that the overwhelming reality of a summer day in the desert is searing heat. But it isn't the triple-digit temperature, it's the observation that *all* of my thoughts have to do with it that engages my attention.

There are a lot of things to look at and innumerable things to ponder so why am I not spending my mental energy on those? I mean, there's nothing I can do to make the heat go away, so why am I spending all my time thinking about it? This puts me in the odd state of thinking about my thinking so I decide to think about that oddity for a while, which means that now I'm thinking about the fact that I'm thinking about my thinking. I end up wondering how many levels of thinking it's possible to think about. Theoretically, it's endless. But if you go down that road, where do you end up? Yep, right back in the searing heat on the straight-as-an-arrow Highway 50.

All that thinking was hard work and it made me hotter than I was before. In fact, I'm now so hot that I'm getting delirious and begin to wonder if maybe all that thinking was wrongheaded. In other words, maybe it's actually cool and I'm the only one who thinks it's hot. I mean, there are probably millions of lizards who think the weather is just peachy. Snakes and beetles, too. So why do I think it's so hot when they don't? I'd been thinking about all this for a while when finally – finally! – another thought enters my overheated consciousness: Perception is reality.

Perception is reality. I don't know who first came up with that saying, but I do know that when I first heard it, I railed against it. I didn't like the concept and I disliked even more when others agreed with it. I wanted truth; I was young and yearned for it. Hell, I'm not young now and I *still* want truth. It wasn't until years later that I realized that reality and truth are not synonymous. Not even close. Put another way, even if we accept the premise that perception *is* reality, it doesn't make that reality actually true, even if it's a reality shared by billions. Truth and reality are two different things, two different concepts.

When you listen to reporters and commentators talk about the news, especially politics and politicians, "perception is reality" sometimes pops up. And when it does, it often comes across as an excuse. Perhaps the reason for this argument, or excuse, is that coming up with a perception and making it a reality is easy; it takes no skill at all, no effort, no adherence to a higher calling. In fact, getting a perception is part of any existence anywhere, and it's something that's impossible to avoid. Even a single cell in a wooly mammoth's curly tusk got perceptions and subsequent realities.

On the other hand, finding truth *does* require some skill, occasionally an effort, and a steadfast adherence to a higher calling, requirements that are, evidently, not expected when talking about politics and politicians.

Now, I've heard that when someone goes into a high meditative state, they're not aware of anything, that it's just an infinite expanse of nothingness. That may be true, I don't have a personal knowledge of it, but I'm willing to accept the word of someone who's been there. Then again, you could make an argument that the awareness of a nothingness *is* a perception. Just because nothing is there doesn't negate the fact that one is *perceiving* that nothing is there. But that might be nothing more than an intellectual exercise that doesn't really get to the truth of the matter. Again, I don't know.

The seeming impossibility of living without getting perceptions and creating realities from them leads me to try and figure out a circumstance in which I could avoid creating realities and still be alive, a mental exercise that leads me nowhere, which is similar to the way I'm feeling while riding on the Loneliest Road in America.

It's time to be truthful about Highway 50. The truth of it, *not* the reality, is that I've been a little harsh regarding that tough asphalt gentleman.

There's an at-a-distance beauty to the desert of Nevada, an inviting vacancy, an untamed aesthetic, and Highway 50 is a perfect place to see it. Just being here gives you a tough serenity. And the straight-as-an-arrow comment I made earlier was only my delirious reality at the time. In other words, it's not the truth. Sure, there are long, straight stretches but it also meanders lazily through occasional hills and sparse greenery and sits under terrific sky.

From a first glance, the desert towns seem spare but the friendliness of the people living in them isn't. Except for one instance, everyone I meet is eager to talk, eager to help and makes me feel welcome. The one exception is at a hotel in Eureka. I had thought to rent a room for a short snooze then continue on my way, but the woman behind the desk, who refuses to look at me directly, says there is nothing available, which can't be true because the place has at least fifty rooms and there are only three cars in the parking lot. When I begin to explain that I need only a couple of hours of sleep, she mumbles something about it being a family place then walks away.

So I go across the street, buy a vanilla ice cream cone and eat it while sitting on a sidewalk bench facing the lady at the hotel desk. Then I buy another one and do the same thing. I don't know if this is bothering her but I like to think she's at least thinking about her attitude. But she's the only sour person I meet. Everyone else I speak with is the opposite, especially the two ladies who own the ice cream shop. They're a lot more pretty, too, so I walk back in and have a nice chat. Then it's time to go.

Not long after leaving Eureka, Highway 50 begins to get a little hilly and it is pleasant, the main reason being that it's less hot. It's not a lush area by anyone's estimation but at least the small amount of vegetation is green and growing. Along this stretch is where I come upon four delays due to road construction. At one of them, I pull up alongside Eric the ex-cop from Emmit, Indiana and his Road King. (He mumbles a bit when we introduce ourselves so I'm not sure Emmit, Indiana is what he says, but it *is* what I hear. Possibly another Reality verses Truth moment.) We have a nice chat, mostly about family and kids. He tells me he's on his way home after visiting his son in Oregon and I tell him about the birthday party in Colorado. It's when I mention how many miles I'd covered without any rest that he puts on his cop face and assumes his cop voice. "Don't ride when you're tired. Just pull over and take a nap." I appreciate his concern, I really do.

I arrive in Ely (EE-lee) in the afternoon and enjoy a few hours of deep sleep in a campground. When my alarm rudely wakes me up, I think about sleeping a couple of more hours then photographing the sunset, but it's an idea from a lazy mind. I need to keep getting in miles. Before and after Ely, the land goes back and forth between hilly and flat, the flat parts similar to the former dryness and at-a-distance beauty with the scabbed mountains far off in the distance. Once, it even rains for about thirty minutes. As the sunlight wanes, about thirty-five miles before the Utah border, I pull over to the side of the road. There's no turnout or anything but there isn't any traffic either so I figure it's safe enough. I just want to smoke a cigarette and enjoy the early evening for a few minutes.

I feel a Presence, a Mountain Presence, casually friendly, but when I pull out a cigarette I feel a little displeasure coming my way. There's no wind but just as I flick on my lighter, a little gust blows it out. I try the lighter again and the same thing happens. A third time and the same result. I figure the Mountain Presence, for whatever reason, doesn't want anyone smoking in his land but I decide to try a little persuasion. I look around and determine that he's right where you'd expect him to be: in the mountains about 150 yards to my right.

I speak to him, out loud, "Look, it's only a cigarette. I'll be careful. And I won't throw the butt on the ground." (Hey, it's the best persuasive argument I can come up with.) No answer, not even a sigh. I try every technique known to smokers: cupping your hands, turning your back to the wind, bending at the knees, squishing your shoulders, everything. I flick the lighter a fourth, fifth, sixth and seventh time, but every time a gust blows out the flame before I can light my cigarette, and those little gusts arrive *only* when I'm flicking the lighter. I start laughing and ask him to give me a break. He chuckles a bit himself but remains adamant. I unsuccessfully try the lighter two more times and finally throw up my hands and say, "Okay okay, you win!", and put the cigarettes and lighter away. Nevertheless, I so enjoy the subsequent fifteen minutes. In the still and gloaming air, with mountains silhouetted against an indigo sky and utter silence all around, I find a different kind of peace.

When I start up The Beast, I expect to feel a little uneasy when his roar bursts into that wonderful silence. But I don't. Instead, his roar seems natural, like it belongs there. The Mountain Presence may frown on cigarettes but he loves the way The Beast speaks to him.

I spend the night at the Border Inn where I have my first sit-down dinner since Sacramento. The following morning, I leave right after sunrise and see my first sign in the state of Utah: NEXT SERVICES 83 MILES. I'd gassed up the night before (a good policy) so I'm fine with that. (When you're in the desert you don't expect to come across many amenities, especially on the Loneliest Road in America.) At first, it's much like Nevada but then the ol' trusty Highway 50 leads me into some low hills. There isn't much in the way of challenging curves but the at-a-distance beauty is brought up-close, with sparsely vegetated, steep hillsides right next to the road.

I come across some clean, well-ordered farms and a little later I have a tasty lunch at the Rancher Motel-Cafe in the well-ordered town of Delta.

After lunch it's drizzling. When I reach Interstate 15, it's raining heavily and the wind has picked up considerably. I pull over for a few minutes to decide if I should take Interstate 15 south until it meets Interstate 70. It's a safer route but Highway 50 has become an old friend so I stay with him and shun the superslab. The winds grow harder, almost violent, and I feel uncertain on the freshly wet pavement, but I learned long ago to trust The Beast. He can handle it and he did handle it like a champ.

For the whole day, the traffic had been scant enough so that it felt like I was riding alone, that the road belonged only to me. The rain always amplifies this 'alone' feeling (why is that?), which in turn amplifies the number of random thoughts rolling through my consciousness. Like Mark Twain once invented a new kind of suspenders; and Karate was invented in India, not Japan; and when he was president, Franklin Delano Roosevelt used a car that originally belonged to Al Capone. (Why would I even know those things?) And a joke my brother told me when we were kids: French people eat snails because they don't like fast food. And about the crazy things that happen in a forty-mile-deep hole the Russians are digging. It's as if those odd and random thoughts are saying, "Uh, you've been keeping us in here long enough, time to let us go." And what better place to escape to than during a lonely ride in the rain?

Eventually, I roll into Salina, which the locals pronounce sa-LIE-nuh, turn right at the World Famous Mom's Cafe, then roll into a gas station and fill up. When I enter the mini-mart to get some beef jerky, it feels as if I'm seeing other humans for the first time in a long while.

A couple of blocks later I came upon Interstate 70. For two hundred miles, Highway 50 and Interstate 70 are the officially same, but Highway 50 doesn't seem comfortable being a freeway and it seems wrong, almost unkind, to think of him as one. Later on in Grand Junction, Colorado, the two split and Highway 50 again becomes it's own path. It goes south for a while, then heads east again at Montrose and into Kansas City. But because of the separation of those two hundred miles, the Colorado/Kansas 50 is more like a brother to the Nevada/Utah 50 than the same road. Which is the big brother and which is the little brother is up for debate, but I do know this: they're certainly not twins. The 50 ends in Ocean City, Maryland but I've never been on it east of Kansas City, so I've no idea how many siblings there are.

Before getting onto Interstate 70, I park under the overpass – no reason to stand in the rain – and pay my respects to Highway 50, a tip of the helmet as it were. Despite his age and the harsh conditions, he holds the route well and has delivered me safely.

You can quote me on this: there are stretches on Interstate 70 through Eastern Utah and Colorado that are flat out, drop dead, gloriously freakin' beautiful. Really. I can't stop myself from stopping to take photos. I mean, I want to just sit there and stare at it. It's so breathtaking that whenever I turn a corner into a new view I yell "Holy Cannoli!" Except I don't say cannoli. I say one of those words you're not supposed to say in polite company. Not that we're necessarily in polite company here—don't want to lay an unwanted label on anyone—but you know what I mean.

I ride into the night and there's a constant lightning display in front of me that's hundreds of miles wide, so even on a cloud-covered night it's *still* beautiful. Of course, most times lightning means rain and this is no exception. But the two rainstorms I ride through don't dampen the thrill at all. I continue into Colorado and end up staying at The Rusty Cannon in Rifle. Yep, there's actually a motel named The Rusty Cannon in a town called Rifle. What a terrific name for a town! I wish I had been born there so when people ask, "Where ya from, mister?" I could say "Rifle, born and raised." I'd be sunburnt and wearing a sweat-stained cowboy hat, and I'd pronounce it "Rhaful" instead of "Rifle" and say it with that John Wayne fixin'-fer-a-fight look in my eyes. Wouldn't that be great?

Before getting my room, I fill up at the gas station right next to the motel. It's also a convenience store that's conveniently located – what a coincidence! – right off the freeway and the thing that first catches my attention is the name of the place: Kum & Go. Uh … oh-kay. Now, I don't know how long these Kum & Go places have been around or how many of them exist, but as I'm filling my tank with 91 Premium I get to wondering which would be more: the number of times a joke has been made about that name or the number of dollars in the national debt. Probably a tossup. Anyway, I walk up to the counter and the cheerful teenager behind it asks, "What can I do for ya?" Oh, the implications....

The next day, the I-70 continues to be beautiful and beautifully large and I've gotten to the point where I'm pulling off at every exit to take photos. (I've an easy day, fewer than two hundred miles, so I should be okay schedule-wise.) The Rocky Mountains angle into the sky without permission or regret and they do it with a vigorous personality that makes you feel the same. I've always been taken by how the mountains, all of the earth actually but especially the mountains, are unaffected by man's partitions. We and our schemes are transitory but there they patiently sit, undisturbed and unimpressed.

As I continue east, the elevation rises and rises. Just east of Vail I see a sign: VAIL PASS SUMMIT ELEV. 10,603Ft. Right after that is when I realize that all my photo stops have put me in danger of not making it to the birthday party in time. This is also when I get my first lesson about weather in Colorado.

I run into a hellacious rainstorm that feels like someone is shooting a pellet gun into my face. So I pull to the side of the freeway, unsnap the bag, pull out my jacket and my face mask, put on the jacket, take off my helmet, put on my face mask, get my other gloves and put them on along with the helmet, put away my fingerless gloves, snap the bag shut – to paraphrase Hemingway, I'm as frantic as a drunkard opening a case of whiskey – get back on the bike and wait for a break in traffic. Some of the big trucks honk to let me know I'll be splashed with gallons of ice-cold freeway water – thanks fellas! – but it doesn't matter because I'm already soaked to the marrow. I pull back onto the freeway and not a half mile later it stops raining and the sun is brightly shining like it never left. The one good thing about all this is that I got what I call my biker's laundry done. Ride through some rain, then ride when it's not raining. Your clothes get wet, they dry: Biker's Laundry.

About forty miles later I ride through the tile-lined Eisenhower-Johnson Memorial Tunnel, which slips just as trouble-free as can be under the Continental Divide at an elevation over eleven thousand feet. At a mile and a half long, it's the longest tunnel I've ever ridden through. When you're going east, as I am, you're on the Johnson side, going west you're on the Eisenhower side. One remarkable thing is how much colder it is inside the tunnel than outside.

The mountain towns I ride by are clean and spacious and idyllic. Their architecture is exactly what you'd expect of mountain towns: wooden structures, steeply angled roofs, smartly framed windows and all of them painted with either earth colors or bright red. Even though I'm running out of time, I still insist on my Helluvits so I take a side trip through Georgetown. It is so picturesque and perfectly situated between steep cliffs that it seems like it's posing for a photograph for one of those look-how-perfectly-beautiful-this-is jigsaw puzzles.

I descend out of the mountains and finally see Denver. I don't wear a watch but figure that if everything goes right, I'll barely make it to the birthday party in time. However, once I get into the Denver metropolitan area the first thing I do is get lost. But getting lost in a big city is a common occurrence after riding for days on open roads. You get used to the wide-open spaces and going where and when you want at the speed you want. Then, when you get into big city congestions, you feel like a gymnast in a suit of armor that's one size too small.

The traffic is going about 10 mph and I'm anxious. I pull up next to a guy riding a BMW and ask him if lane splitting is legal in Colorado. He says it isn't but to go ahead; he doesn't think I'll get ticketed. So I split lanes for a couple of miles, hoping to see a familiar name on a road sign. (In my rear view mirror, I see the fellow on the Beemer lane-splitting as well.) Eventually, I pull off and get the first of two directions and find out I've gone about ten miles too far.

I get to Jasmine and Omar's house at 5 P.M. on the dot – I made it! – and Omar and his dad, Enrique, drive me over to Chuck E Cheese just in time for Rio's birthday party. I sing with the kids, play some games and have a terrific conversation with one of the mothers about the fact that crude oil is not a fossil fuel. And I eat too much pizza and cake and drink too much soda but, hey, I deserve it.

I spend my six days in Colorado with Jasmine and Omar and Omar's extended family, which is fairly extensive. One day I ride with Omar and Enrique up Highway 72 to Wondervu, which, coincidentally, has a wonderful view, though Wondervu is pronounced WON-der-voo. While I'm eating a seriously tasty Mexican omelet, I realize a fundamentally serious problem with Colorado: there are so, so many wonderful views that it's impossible to take in even six percent of them in six days. It's like going to the Great Barrier Reef and sticking your head under water for only six seconds. You're just not going to get it.

On Monday afternoon I'm taking a nap. I feel my shoulder shaking. I open my eyes and see Travis, Rio and Maya, Rio's six-year-old sister, staring at me. This is *exactly* how it goes down.

Rio: Wanna see my rocks?

Maya: Ewww, rocks are dirty.

Travis: I got a balloon sword!

Gotta love it.

The highlight of my stay is Tuesday. Jasmine is pregnant – she's beautiful! – and I go with her and Omar to the doctor to see the sonogram in real time. My oh my oh my! There's the head, the rump, the arms, the legs, and there's the little heart thumping along at 171 beats per minute. What an amazing technology.

On Wednesday, Travis washes The Beast, which he does every time I visit. He always does a good job and it's something I really appreciate. Afterward, I have him climb on the back and we go for an ice cream. I buy Travis what he wants and, as always, it's much more than he can eat.

Thursday arrives and it's time to leave. Saying goodbye to all these wonderful people is tough so I laze around for hours, do a whole lot of nothing, and it's well into the afternoon before I get on Interstate 25 North. I don't know what lies ahead, but I do know I'm feeling fresh and new, and after the good washing that Travis gave him, The Beast feels the same. The beginning of another Helluvit.

A little ways before the Wyoming border I pull off the freeway to indulge in an agreeable melancholy. I find a solitary field outside of a place called Loveland, a name that perfectly describes my sentiment, and it's here that I let my thoughts and their feelings linger. I remember the conversations over dinner and the singing afterward, the shared dreams and the lame jokes. I remember a trip to the aquarium, toasts to health and prosperity, playing horseshoes, and dipping corn chips into homemade salsa while sipping a gin and tonic. I think about my extended family all of whom have become dear friends as well, about kids and rocks and balloons, about a young couple in love. I think about a little heart beating 171 times a minute.

I'm thrilled to have gotten there on time, a goal achieved as it were, and my stay was pure delight. Yet here I am, thoroughly delighted to be back on the road in a solitary Helluvit. This gets me thinking about having a balance in life. On one side of the balance are our goals, on the other side are our Helluvits. If you never do anything but reach one goal after another, if predetermined goals are *all* you have your attention on, you'll end up with a surface-only life. On the other hand, if you engage in nothing but Helluvits, your life will end up being a confused mess. And at the end of each of those lives you'll be at a loss to answer this simple question: What was it all for? But if you achieve that balance, even if it's only a sometimes occurrence, you'll have more answers than anyone could count.

Shards of sunlight stand upon the earth like grand pillars holding up the clouds while the rich smells of soil and growth intermingle in the shimmering air.

7

DIFFERENT WORLDS

Riding is my hallowed place.
The more I ride, the more I enjoy it;
The more I enjoy it, the more I ride.
My focus is more keen,
My thoughts more definite and swift,
More sacred.

And I change.

I change from being separate-from to being part-of.
I go from a belief that everything will be okay
To a state of being where everything is okay.

I see the constellations continue their morphings;
I rise above and see the earth proudly owning its place in the Milky
Way;
The stars, each lighting its own destiny.
I listen to the wind,
And the heart of the earth beats through me.

—Dwight Bernard Mikkelsen

There's a friendly how-ya-doin' breeze when I cross the border from Minnesota into Wisconsin on US Highway 53. All around me, all

I see, is an organized bustle. I don't know what they grow in Wisconsin but there's a lot of it. The hills are soft with grasses and the fields are miles and miles of thriving green, a luxuriance of prodigal plant life. There is simply not one lifeless spot.

I decide to spend the night in Eau Claire and on the way, I wonder how it's pronounced. Oh Claire? Ooh Claire? Ewww Claire? Ah, Claire? Eclair? Yo, Claire? (I ask the lady at the motel desk, an inveterate reader of novels, and she tells me it's pronounced oh-CLARE.) The following morning I get on Interstate 94 and the how-ya-doin' breeze has turned into a Muhammad Ali smack-you-in-the-face wind that keeps getting stronger and stronger and insanely swirly so by the time I'm forty miles northwest of Madison, I'm thinking I need some Velcro sewn on my butt just to stay in the seat.

I arrive in Madison and my first impression is that it's fundamentally a white-collar place. Except for my motel, which is called something along the lines of Hawaiian Breeze or Palm Tree Paradise. After staying there for only one night, I decide to never again stay at a place with a name that has any reference to an island in the Pacific. While waiting for the desk clerk to get off the phone, something happened that, had I been more survival-minded, told me I shouldn't stay there. The owner is constantly walking an old, grime-covered inexpensive stroller. She's quietly humming an odd melody and occasionally leans over and whispers something sweet. Once, as she walks by, I peek in and nestled in the soft blankets is a small, white bulldog.

I get to my room and lie down on the bed to snooze an hour or so before dinner. I notice a smell. I dislike that: Right before you go to sleep you notice something, like the ticking of a clock or your heartbeat pulsing in your left big toe, and it keeps you awake no matter how hard you try and ignore it. In fact, the more you try and ignore it, the more it keeps you awake. It's like mental caffeine. That's the way it is with the smell; the more I smell it, the worse it gets, and the more I'm awake. And it smells nothing at all like a cup of freshly brewed coffee, but more like an alien reptile decomposing in a warm oven. I get up to open the window but, wouldn't you know it, it's nailed shut.

I lie down again and have another go at ignoring the smell. It doesn't work. Soon, the mental caffeine kicks in and I begin to think that a smell that unusual, that vile, must be some kind of biohazard, like it'll make my skin peel off or turn my hair into a bunch of purple eggplants. I get up and look out the door, the peephole of which is just that: a hole with no metal or glass. I walk out into the hallway and there's no smell. I walk back in and my eyes begin to water and my breathing is choked. I check the window again but it's definitely nailed shut for good. I look under the bed, under the sink and behind the chest of drawers, even open all the drawers, but nothing.

Finally, I look into the bathroom and, aha!, there's a big blue bucket next to the toilet. I bend over and, ouch!, this is it. From the look and smell of it, the blue bucket is there to catch leaks from the toilet upstairs, which it's obviously been doing for a long time because it's filled almost to the brim. I lift it (it's heavy) and pour the dark liquid into the bathtub but the bottom third is this thick, multi-colored slime that's stuck to the bucket like warm taffy. I nearly pass out. I barely manage to turn on the shower and barely manage to wait five minutes for the hot water. Finally, I can rinse out the bucket. Ah, much better! At least now I can sleep a few winks and not have a bunch of purple eggplants sticking out of my head.

Madison is one of only four state capitals with the same name as a US president. (At least until we elect someone named Tallahassee or Saint Paul.) Now, you might think that this is an essentially useless fact, but consider this: Say you're hanging out with your friends and casually state this fact and say none of your friends know it, why you'll be a mini-celebrity until the next round of beers. See? It does have a use! (By the bye, the other three are Lincoln, Nebraska; Jefferson City, Missouri; and Jackson, Mississippi.) My motel room notwithstanding, I find Madison to be a clean and well-trimmed city. As I said, it seems to be fundamentally white-collar, but I soon discover this whole University-Town element to it. Then, the more I see of it, the more I find an old-time, well-mannered ambience as well.

There are a lot of coffee shops and pubs and they all seem to be "in the back and up the stairs." I picture university students staying up all night drinking Jaegermeister and coffee while arguing the virtues and evils of Milton Friedman and John Keynes. Flashing eyes, table pounding, name calling, the works. All this while my friend, Mars, and I celebrate her birthday with a fabulous dinner at Lao Laan-Xang – sorry, I've no idea how to pronounce it –, which is an authentically appointed Laotian place, sidewalk seating, and I overhear the people at the table next to us arguing the fine points of Italian wines.

Mars takes me on a mini-tour of Madison and I see people walking their dogs and families riding bicycles together. (Bike lanes are everywhere.) There are old and arched, whitewashed bridges over the numerous streams and small rivers. Residents sit on their porches in front of aged but well-kept, wooden two-story houses watching the moon settle over the three bigger lakes (Mendota, Monona and Waubesa) or one of the many smaller ones. The capital building is immaculately lit, the streets are litter-free, and the citizens amble about as if there's not a pickpocket in the county.

I make it back to my motel room and the smell is still gone, thank goodness. I check the blue bucket and it's still empty. More thank goodness. But I've come to not trust the place so I sleep in my clothes and boots on top of the bed cover, and use my jacket for a pillow. Before falling asleep I think about Madison. It seems that in just one day I've come to know it so well. But then, a transient visitor will never know a town really well. You'd have to be a permanent resident to do that. But even then, do any of us ever truly and fully know a city? All of its shortcomings and all of its assets? All of its squalor and all of its beauty? Of course not. We can't. Those things are changing constantly. It occurs to me that we measure our knowledge of towns and cities not by how many people we know, not by how many street names we know, not by how many historical facts we know, but by how comfortable we are when we're there. And I'm comfortable in Madison, my motel room notwithstanding.

The following day I discover a grand dichotomy. I leave Madison and ride seventy-five miles west on Interstate 94 to Milwaukee, the home of a fabulous blue-collar, working-town, no-apologies attitude. It's also home to the Harley-Davidson Museum where I arrive just in time to take a tour of the plant where they make the power trains (engines and transmissions) and it's the best thing ever. In the museum itself there's a Harley scooter (yes, a red Harley scooter), a Harley golf cart, one of Elvis's Harleys, a six-cylinder Harley, a mail carrier Harley, Harley bicycles, and samples of all the Harleys since 1903. And I find out that back in the 1930s, the famous woman biker, Dot Robinson, had a lipstick holder on her Harley. While looking at the pictures of Dot, I try and remember if I've ever seen a woman, any woman, on a motorcycle that wasn't incredibly sexy. I can't.

The white-collar/blue-collar dichotomy between Madison and Milwaukee is distinct but there's another interesting contrast. If you're over eighteen in Wisconsin, you're not required by law to wear a helmet. However, many of the riders in Madison are helmet wearers but almost none in Milwaukee wear one. I'm standing outside the museum wondering why this is when Dale, a Wisconsin resident, a biker, and a long-distance truck driver, walks up and starts a conversation. He says he's noticed this difference before but doesn't know why it's like that, either. Then he adds that most of the Milwaukee cops are riders and even if there was a helmet law, they'd probably ignore it. I love that!

Before I go back to my motel, which is inexpensive but a pretty nice place anyway (clean pool, weight room, and lots of well-stocked vending machines), I take a ride into and around the suburb Wauwatosa. In a way, it's typically suburban: The de rigueur golf course, activity center and playgrounds are there along with all the typical chain restaurants. There are new and large corner gas stations, small strip malls and medium-sized malls but I don't see one of those gargantuan malls, though I'm sure there must be one around here some place. On the other hand, I occasionally see a mom-and-pop place tucked away behind some trees. I can tell that many of the neighborhoods were built in the pre-typical-suburban era because of the architecture and the fact that the roads have been resurfaced many times. It's a unique and rustic flavor.

There's a blue-collar restaurant next to my motel called the Country Spring Restaurant. This one, like many other blue-collar restaurants, strikes me as having been at one time a serve-yourself cafeteria. I walk in and decide to splurge on a steak dinner. Just as I finish my steak, Sandy the Blue-Collar Waitress, comes over.

Sandy the Blue-Collar Waitress: How was it?

Me: 'S great!

Sandy the Blue-Collar Waitress: Anything else?

Me: Love a piece of cherry pie.

Sandy the Blue-Collar Waitress: Pie?

Me: Yeah!

Sandy the Blue-Collar Waitress: You want pie?

Me: Uh … yeah…

Sandy the Blue-Collar Waitress: *(Firm gaze, left hand on hip, right hand on table, head cocked to her right)* Mmm … didja eat your vegetables?

Me: Yeah! Well … sort of …

Sandy the Blue-Collar Waitress: *(Raises eyebrows)* Yeah, well, sort of?

Me: Yeah. I ate a slice of carrot and one of those green things.

Sandy the Blue-Collar Waitress: A slice of carrot and one of those green things.

Me: Yeah!

Sandy the Blue-Collar Waitress: And for that you want a piece of pie?

Me: Uh, you know, I just thought … you know …

Sandy the Blue-Collar Waitress: Hmm. *(Puts the bowl of vegetables back in front of me)* Eat your vegetables then we'll talk about pie. *(She walks away)*

So I eat my vegetables, begrudgingly, and finally get my cherry pie, which I eat enthusiastically. Then, without even asking, Sandy brings me a second piece and doesn't charge me for it. Hands down, she gets my vote for Waitress-Mom of the Year.

Before I leave Milwaukee, I ride down to the shores of Lake Michigan. I'm excited because this particular trip was my first to any of the Great Lakes. A week earlier I had been in Minnesota and took a lot of photos of Lake Superior where the endless blue of the lake and the endlessly blue sky cuddle up in the distance. In a way, a metaphorical way, my memory of Lake Superior reminds me of Madison. The sky was perfect, the breezes were perfectly refreshing, and the small, well-behaved waves lapped the rocks as if to say, "My, what a lovely day for a picnic."

Well, if Lake Superior is a metaphorical Madison, Lake Michigan is Milwaukee. The waves are actually up to two feet high and crash, unapologetically, on rocky shores; the clouds glare at you like Vince Lombardi after a three-game losing streak; and as you look out, this is unmistakable, the middle of the lake is *higher* than the shore so you get the feeling that there's a sleeping leviathan right under the surface.

After I finish taking my photos, I stand on the sand thinking about Madison and Milwaukee, two large cities separated by only seventy-five miles of freeway, only one hour, yet it's like they're different worlds, one a dichotomy to the other. In the same way, you could say we each represent some sort of dichotomy to everyone else, that we each have our own world that we live in. There is truth to that, but it's not the complete truth. It's not the complete truth because we all *do share* a common world, just as Madison and Milwaukee share a state. We all reside on the same coin, so to speak, albeit sometimes on different sides, just as Madison and Milwaukee reside on different sides of that seventy-five-mile stretch of Interstate 94.

Then there are the innumerable similarities to consider. Years ago, I adopted the belief that if we all concentrated on our similarities, not our differences, the world would be much better off. I don't know who first came up with this idea but I do know that many, many before me have claimed the wisdom of it. And there is wisdom in it, to be sure, but it's not the only wisdom there is concerning human interaction.

Madison and Milwaukee illustrate another wisdom, every bit as valuable, and that is acknowledging the differences we have with others. The way some act, you'd think that differences necessarily lead to rancor and hostilities. But why? Think about it: What natural law or system of logic demands that we must be hostile to those who are different? There isn't one. If one existed, we'd be in terrible shape, maybe even extinct, because, let's face it, everyone *is* different from everyone else, and each person does represent a dichotomy. Truly, differences with others mean *nothing* other than we have differences. What we do with them is our choice.

Far above is another metaphor: white clouds/blue sky, white-collar/ blue-collar, Madison/Milwaukee.

8

STURGIS: BEFORE, DURING, and BEYOND

RIDING TO STURGIS

I love being on the road. Trail mix for breakfast, beef jerky for lunch, and for dinner you treat yourself to a delicious meal of two corn dogs with cheap yellow mustard. (Please, none of that Grey Poupon stuff.) And there's something special about Barq's Root Beer after a full day of riding. For washing away the dust and the heat and the aching stiffness, and getting you ready for tomorrow, it's far superior to a fine French champagne.

But then, things other than wondrous do happen. Unexpected things. Challenging things.

It was classic mis-planning. There isn't much room on The Beast so I pack only those things I absolutely need, and I'm meticulous about every detail. Things like packing the blue toothbrush instead of the red one because it's smaller. I even make lists. (Imagine!) Once everything is laid out, I quickly get it all packed and strapped down. I stand back and take a look at my handiwork. It's perfect. I'm proud of myself for how I paid attention to everything it's possible to pay attention to.

It's a late start but I'm all excited anyway. I roll out of the driveway, ride the short distance to Interstate 210, head east, then hang a left on Interstate 15 to Las Vegas. Everything is just fine, splendid even. Then, not long after Victorville, a severe reality hits me with a wallop. I'd spent so much time planning the small things that I never thought about one really big one: the torture of riding through the Mojave Desert in the middle of the day in the middle of summer. Take it from me, this is not wise.

One guy tells me the temperature is 118 degrees. (Ouch!) It's so hot, there are times when I'm overcome with ecstasy just from seeing something that looks like a memory of a shadow. It's so hot, my kickstand digs a two-inch hole in the asphalt. It's so hot, the simple act of breathing is like washing my mouth out with the oil leaking out of an overheated '48 Harley Panhead. When I pull into a gas station in Baker and stand up, my head starts swirling so badly I nearly pass out and I have to sit on the gas pump island for five minutes to collect my wits. (I know what you're thinking: Riding through the Mojave Desert in the middle of the day in the middle of summer means I don't have very many wits to collect in the first place. And you're right!)

It doesn't make sense. I'm doing what you're supposed to do: drinking gallons of water and consuming so much potassium I might as well mainline it. So I call a good friend who knows everything in the world about nutrition and tell her the situation. Sally tells me that I have to balance the potassium with salt, that my sodium level is low. "SALT! SALT! SALT!" is the way she puts it. She then tells me that celery is an excellent source of sodium, but celery is a vegetable and I'm not too keen vegetables, so instead, I chow down a big bag of Fritos and thirty minutes later I'm fine.

Right after sunset, I'm in North Las Vegas filling up my tank and ask a road worker, who's doing the same, if he knows of any cheap motels around. He tells me to backtrack down the I-15, get off on Cheyenne and go to the Lucky Club. It's only one exit away and the rooms are only twenty-nine bucks. Sounds good.

Well, there's road construction and my side of the freeway is down to one lane. There was also a fender bender so the highway patrol guys are everywhere, which means I can't split lanes because that's illegal in Nevada. So here I am, enveloped in a lovely bouquet of exhaust fumes and inching along at fifteen feet a minute. My left hand is cramping from constantly working the clutch and I'm covered with a layer of smelly, dried sweat an inch thick. And wouldn't you know it (I'm not making this up) I'm stuck behind a double-trailer truck carrying living, snorting hogs long distance from Utah. I take it as a challenge: Can I find a silver lining in this cloud of hog stench I'm following? Finally, it comes to me. There is, indeed, something on this freeway that smells worse than me.

The following morning I continue on the I-15. About twenty-five miles southwest of St. George, as I'm slicing across the northwestern corner of Arizona, the desert finally gives way to some nice canyons and the freeway swoops through them just as nice as you please. And, thank goodness, the air is a bit cooler. I spend the night in Salt Lake City and it surprises me a little. For some reason, I'd always had the image of it being a drab and boring place but it's not.

The next day, I ride through sprawling, windswept Wyoming where all the roads lead through nowhere but they all end up somewhere. It seems like all the cattle are grass-fed and the billions of insects I was expecting are on vacation. I spend the night in Casper and the next day stop to fill up in Midwest, which has a population of 404, one gas station, one pump, and I don't know how many grass-fed cattle or insects. I head north on Highway 50 and at Gillette take Interstate 90 East. Here, finally, is where the countryside gradually gets greener. By now, there are more motorcycles than cars and you can feel and hear the excitement in the air. But there's something else, something magical, something sacred. I'm heading into the soul-filled Black Hills, the place the Sioux called The Heart of All Things.

The Black Hills Motorcycle Rally in Sturgis (central-western South Dakota) is the largest motorcycle rally in the world. No one is certain of the exact numbers but in 2011, there were about 415,000 attendees. But that's just Sturgis. If you count the entire rally, which includes Spearfish, Rapid City, Deadwood, Keystone, Lead, and a few others, there were easily over a half million. Add to that 955 vendors, fifty-nine marriage licenses, over a million pounds of garbage, and over eleven million dollars in taxes and we're talking one BIG party. The people I spoke with were expecting (or hoping for or afraid of, depending on their viewpoint) as much as a thirty percent increase this year.

Riding to Sturgis is like a pilgrimage in the religion of Bikerdom. Everywhere you stop, you see other bikers and toward the beginning of your journey the conversations go something like this.

"How ya doin."

"How do."

"Sturgis?"

"Yep."

"Me too." *(Long, satisfying sigh)* "Beautiful day, ain't it."

"It is that." *(pause)* "Hot, though."

"Tell ya what."

By the time you're within two or three hundred miles of Sturgis, everyone makes the valid assumption that if you're on a bike, you *must* be going to the Black Hills Motorcycle Rally, so the conversations change a bit.

"How ya doin'?"

"How do."

"Where ya stayin'?"

"The Chip. You?"

"Lamphere. Prolly see ya around."

"Buy ya a beer." *(Long, satisfying sigh)*

"Beautiful day, ain't it."

"It is that." *(pause)*

"Hot, though."

"Tell ya what."

It's a laconic exchange but embedded in it is a deep philosophy of brother- and sisterhood.

I love bikers. I passed one guy who was cruising around 60 mph on a decades-old Electra Glide, and on the seat behind him was an old hound dog wearing goggles. Some guys in St. George told me that a biker and his lady won $180,000 when they stopped in Las Vegas and they're giving $100 to everyone they meet who is riding to Sturgis. (I missed them by fifteen minutes.) I told the desk lady, who's a rider, at the Motel 6 in Salt Lake City that I wanted a room on the bottom floor. There weren't any available but she moved the people with a reservation up to the second floor and gave me their first floor room. At the motel in Casper, the bikers in the two rooms above me were carrying on a loud and rowdy party. The Olympics were on their TV and when the Star Spangled Banner came on, they all quit partying and listened reverently. Later that night, they even sang along, probably had their hands over their hearts, too.

SURVIVING STURGIS

After 1,392 miles, I arrive in Sturgis on Saturday at 3:30 P.M. The town itself has a population of only 6,627 and is only six blocks long, but there are so many motorcycles that it takes me over an hour just to get through it. At the Buffalo Chip Campground, my home for the next week, the first thing I see is the Moving Wall Vietnam War Memorial, at the front of which are hundreds and hundreds of American flags waving in the breeze. The sight fills my heart. Despite the dozen, well-informed and efficient check-in girls, it takes another hour to check in. The one who checks me in is tired, hot and over-worked.

Me: So is there a specific area or place for me to go?

Tired, Hot and Over-worked Check-in Girl: Watcha got?

Me: A bike and a tent.

Tired, Hot and Over-worked Check-in Girl: Jus' wherever y'can find a spot.

So I ride into the campground to find a spot. It's enormous. 560 acres of nearly flat land covered with grass (that'd be prairie grass, not lawn grass) and there might be a tree or two, I don't know. There are already thousands of motorhomes, trailers, campers, RVs, ATVs, and countless motorcycles. And beer. Lots of beer. Yep, the official start of the Black Hills Motorcycle Rally is still two days away and already the partying has begun.

I finally find my spot toward the northwest corner above what looks like an old drainage ditch. It's here that I will soon learn the fine art of dressing and undressing in a small tent. The neighbors on my right are Brad and Mitchell from Nevada, and on my left are Duane and Cameron. Duane lives in Texas and Cameron in Oklahoma but they were high school buddies in Nebraska back in the '60s and '70s. Good guys, all four.

I'm tired so my plan is to just set up my tent and relax and sleep until the next day, but around 10:30 P.M. I hear the unbelievably loud roar of the crowd at the concert and decide to investigate. After walking for what seems like miles I get to the concert area and it's amazing. Thousands of people, standing room only, and on the Wolfman Jack Stage, Zac Brown is flat out rockin' the place. He's on top of his game, the band is tight and the sound is loud and perfect. He leads the entire crowd in a prayer for the safety of all our troops and there isn't a dry eye in the place. Then he goes into a beautiful rendition of *America, the Beautiful*. And it is beautiful. But the crowd makes it Sturgis-unique with their running commentary.

O beautiful for spacious skies ... FUCKIN' LOVE THIS COUNTRY!

... America! America! ... THESE COLORS DON'T RUN MOTHERFUCKER!

And on and on. When he kicks into *Chicken Fried*, the partying kicks up a notch and the whole place makes the Super Bowl look like a Sunday brunch in a retirement home.

I get back to my tent and crawl into my sleeping bag around 1 A.M., and on the following day I go into town.

Sturgis. It's a place where cars are not allowed on Main Street, as it should be; a place where pedestrians yield their right-of-way to motorcycles, as they should; a place where the throaty din of thousands of motorcycles is as welcomed as a mother's lullaby, as it should be. It's a place where the men walk with a gunfighter's swagger but act like chivalrous knights; never mind the old t-shirts, crumpled jeans and dust-covered boots. It's a place where the ladies act and are treated like noblewomen, though some are wearing body paint instead of bras and tops, and others are dressed like leather-clad harlots, age and size and shape notwithstanding.

It's a place that's infused with that Midwestern hospitality of charm, understated humor, and non-judgmental nature. It's a place where you see flags from all over the world: Canada, France, England, Germany, Scandinavia, Australia, South Africa, Mexico, and dozens of others. But the one you see most often has red stripes and white stars. Old Glory never looked more at home.

It's a place where the two most common names are Jack and Daniel. It's a place with saloons named EasyRiders, Full Throttle, Side Hack, Broken

Spoke, and Knuckle, and I visited all of 'em. It's a place where paying for dinner will have you dipping into your IRA account, but you can buy all the leather and jewelry you want with the few bills in your pocket. It's a place where the Country Rock is loud, the Hard Rock is louder, the Heavy Metal is louder still, but the loudest of all is the constant, and I mean every-second-of-the-day-and-night constant, howling rumble of motorcycles. The big bikes, the bad boy bikes, the man bikes, the bikes from hell that take you straight to heaven.

I'm on Lazelle Street and it's packed; rear-to-front fender, two bikes side-by-side in each of the four lanes. The pedestrians are moving four times faster than we are. There's a guy hawking some sort of something on a loudspeaker (motorcycle insurance or motorcycle oil or whatever) but no one's paying attention. So he asks, "Anyone with loud pipes out there?" All of us, hundreds of us, immediately roll on our throttles like we're dying of thirst and twisting the top off of the last beer bottle on the planet. It's so loud it's painful, and I'm deaf in one ear. It's so loud that politicians ten miles away are calling the National Guard. It's so loud I think the earth itself is going crack open and we'll all fall into the center and shake hands with Jules Verne himself.

While walking around and taking photos of the more unusual bikes, I overhear some snippets of conversations:

- Whaddya mean I can't get a beer at ten o' clock on a Sunday morning. Is this a bike rally or what!
- Y'know what's wrong with all that Rap and Hip Hop crap? It's all about the buck and not about the fuck.
- We walked and hitchhiked all the way from Tennessee. Took us seventy-three days. (Her companion was a small, brown and white pooch.)
- If you do the titty thang I'll do the pumpkin thang.
- There's two types of runnin': away and to. Y'can tell which it is by the look in their eyes.
- Too many damn bikes!
- Too much damn dirt!
- Not enough women!
- There ain't never too much beer!

Worried about safety? Sure, bad things happen. Get a half million strangers partying together for almost two weeks and it'll all happen: property damage, divorce and death. (In 2011, there were four rally-related deaths, which is an impressively low number considering that many people.) On the other hand, there are those who'll spend hours fixing a stranger's bike for nothing more than a "thank you," and those who fall in love and get married. And there are those, believe it or not, who give birth to healthy and beautiful biker babies.

During the entire rally, I never heard a gun fired and never saw anyone pull out a knife. I never saw a fight or an argument, and the only unkind words I heard were between two vendors. I had nothing stolen or destroyed or defaced. In fact, I locked up my bike only once, and that was on the first day. By actual statistics, the Black Hills Motorcycle Rally is safer than eighty-eight percent of the rest of the country. Truly, the entire time I felt as safe as I would eating a steak and lobster dinner in a five-star restaurant in Switzerland.

The thing is, if you like who you are and how you look, you'll like Sturgis. If you like honest laughter and big-hearted strangers, you'll like Sturgis. If you like unblemished good company and good times, you'll like Sturgis. If you like music and freedom and the United States of America, you'll like Sturgis. It's life, all of life, right there out in the open, and if you love life and all who participate in it, you'll love Sturgis.

On Sunday afternoon and evening, I mostly hang out with my neighbors. One couple is from Connecticut and another from Florida; the others from everywhere in the Midwest. That night we all sit around and tell stories and laugh. It's interesting that the one topic not brought up is politics, which I find refreshing.

On Monday, I take a ride up to Mt. Rushmore. The thing that impresses me most is the well-defined and accurate representation of the four faces: Washington, Jefferson, Lincoln and Teddy Roosevelt. (I swear, at a certain angle, Teddy has a grin on his face like he just put a whoopee cushion on Lincoln's chair.) It's sixty miles away from Sturgis yet three-quarters of the parking lot is reserved for motorcycles. (During the Sturgis rally, an average of six thousand bikers visit each day.) Afterward, I head over to the yet unfinished Crazy Horse Monument, which is so huge it makes Mt Rushmore look like a Christmas tree ornament. I then take Highway 385 through the heart of the Black Hills and what a magical and magically pretty place it is. I rest a while in Deadwood at the Silverado Casino where I lose $20 playing video poker while the guy next to me, a rider from Ohio, wins over $200.

That night I go to the Journey concert instead of going to see Travis Tritt. It's a mistake. The new singer and drummer do a fine job but the other three members (guitar, bass and keyboards) don't really connect with the audience. And their playing is a bit sloppy and they make a lot of mistakes. The guitar player even gets lost during the Star Spangled Banner, which is unforgivable. (But then, I'd been partying so maybe my ability to judge was compromised.) Nevertheless, the crowd itself is forgiving and there are big smiles all around, especially when everyone sings along with *Don't Stop Believin'*.

Wednesday night, I go to the Boston concert. They, too, don't seem to really connect but at least they play well, even showing some excellent chops, which is something I appreciate.

Thursday is pretty much a wander-around-and-take-a-shower day. After days of searching, I finally locate Bikini Beach, which I'm told could sometimes be called Half-Bikini Beach and at other times Where'd-All-Those-Bikinis-Go? Beach. All I saw were full complement bikinis so I don't know if it's ever like that or if it's just wishful fantasizing. My neighbors, Duane and Cameron, left for home and are replaced by a family from Nebraska. They have everything: a mobile home, a trailer, two ATVs, three Harleys, four ice chests, and a propane barbecue. That night, the mother invites me to share a beef brisket dinner with homemade potato salad and it's damn tasty.

Afterward, I have a tough decision: Stay at the Buffalo Chip for the Sugarland/Lynyrd Skynyrd concert or ride over to the Full Throttle Saloon to see Tanya Tucker. I flip the proverbial coin and end up staying at the Chip. Not so much because of the coin flip but because I'd already had a few beers and didn't want to ride in that condition. (Hey, I admit I'm an easy drunk; half a beer gives me a buzz that lasts for hours.)

With a couple of dozen others, I climb on the back of an old hay truck and fifteen minutes later we're walking into the concert area where Sugarland is rocking the house. Afterward, Lynyrd Skynyrd flat out brings it down. They play each tune like it was meant to be played, like it's the last time it'll ever be played. Non-stop exhilaration. Around midnight, the concert is over (the encore is still to come) and after who-knows-how-many-minutes of hooting and hollering and stomping and applauding, the conversation starts.

Lynyrd Skynyrd Fan: Hey, they didn't play *Free Bird*.

Me: They will.

Another Lynyrd Skynyrd Fan: Why didn't they play *Free Bird*?

Me: They will.

Another Lynyrd Skynyrd Fan: I wanna hear *Free Bird*!

Me: You will.

Another Lynyrd Skynyrd Fan: They gotta play *Free Bird*!

Me: They will. If they don't there'll be a riot.

All Lynyrd Skynyrd Fans: *Free Bird, Free Bird, Free Bird!* (*It goes on and on for minutes.*)

Finally, Lynyrd Skynyrd comes back on stage for their encore and, yep, it's *Free Bird*. Like I've never heard it. Like no one's ever heard it. Like no one will ever hear it again. The soundman turns it up then turns it up some more and the jam at the end goes stratospheric. Everyone is dancing and hugging and kissing and flying straight up with them.

On Friday night I go over to the Full Throttle Saloon. Oh Oh Oh! It's advertised as the largest biker bar in the world and I don't doubt it. It's decorated with scores of old motorcycles and cars and trucks and everything blue-collar. In the first section is a very loud three-piece metal band and they are damn good. There's even some head-banging going on. The second section is the very loud DJ part, replete with a huge rectangular bar in the middle with pole dancers. The third section is where the very loud motorcycles can park (yes, they invite motorcycles into the place) and it's where the very loud big-name concerts are held. Then there's the second floor. Surrounding the whole area are dozens of food and souvenir vendors.

Without a doubt, the Full Throttle is the best partying spot I've ever been to. The scantily-clad ladies are looking fine, even the ones weighing over two hundred pounds, and their men are happy to show them off.

I meet farmers from Nebraska, business people from Pennsylvania and a dentist from Arizona. I see Santa Claus, Elvis, a leprechaun, a dog wearing leather chaps and goggles, and a guy carrying a pet duck in a purse. I'm not surprised by any of them. When it's time for the main concert, I go down to the open area and lean against an old Chevy pickup while listening to Molly Hatchet tear it up. What a great thing to do! Even though I'm missing the Slash/Skid Row concert, I cannot be happier.

It had been raining heavily for a quite a while and when I get back, most of my stuff is wet. Even part of my sleeping bag. I swear, the standing water at the back end of my tent is deep enough for bass fishing. I immediately come to the firm belief that the concept of "dry" cannot be overrated. (A piece of advice: Never buy a cheap tent.) I manage to sleep through the night, sort of, and surprisingly wake up Saturday morning without a hangover. I check the weather app on my phone and it says it's going to rain even harder that night. I look at my stuff and wonder how long it takes for mildew to set in. I then experience a few moments of common sense and decide to pack up and leave a day early.

I ride into town to get a few more souvenirs and look around one last time. I'm sad. I don't want to leave. I just don't. The idea of it is tearing me up. When the three best kids in the world (love you Khalin, Lacee and Jasmine!) all tell me to stay, I decide to do just that. Damn the rain and mildew! As I've said before, within the concept of freedom, there is no guarantee of comfort.

That night, as the weather app predicted, it rains even harder and the Sublime concert is cancelled. I'm in the concert area, standing under a metal awning eating a buffalo burrito, when a petite, gum-chewing twenty-something girl from the loud DJ club upstairs walks up and asks to use my phone. She's wearing nothing but fishnets, spike heels, I-don't-know-what in her hair, and three pieces of cloth that are the size of two small post-it notes and an eye patch. I dial the number for her (it's written on the inside of her right forearm) and hand her the phone. She talks a while then hands back my phone and says, "Me-n-my-friends-r-gonna-party-wanna-come?" She opens her hand and shows me three capsules. Two look ominous. The third one is purple. She's thinking it's going to be the best thing ever. I'm thinking I'd have a heart attack before getting to any of the good stuff. So I say, "I do appreciate the invitation but I believe I'll have to decline."

I end the night with a long conversation with a few locals and around 1 A.M., go back to my tent, happy in the belief that my heart will still be beating tomorrow.

Despite my rain soaked surroundings, I sleep well and wake up late. Around noon, I crawl out and see that most of my neighbors have already left. I take a long look around, a full 360-degree view, and breath deeply the rich air. I am sated, sated with friendship and good times and enduring memories. I pack up, load up and leave in the early afternoon, heading east on Highway 34 in front of a northwest wind. Along with the rumbling of my beloved bike, *Free Bird* is vibrating to my core. In my rearview mirror I take one last look at the Buffalo Chip Campground and smile. Twenty minutes later, the South Dakota sun has dried out my boots, jeans, gloves, t-shirt and vest. The last of Sturgis is gone.

But the memories. Oh, the memories…

BEYOND STURGIS

The first order of business I have (actually, the only order of business I have) is to replace the power adaptor for my Mac laptop because the rain in Sturgis had shorted it out. I figure I'll just keep going east on Highway 34 and buy one in Pierre, the capitol of South Dakota. It's only 175 miles away, which means I'll get there with enough time to get caught up on my emails.

The land itself in South Dakota stays pretty much the same throughout: undulating ground covered with prairie grass. Though the road has been patched up a number of times and looks like it'd be bumpy, it's quite smooth. The air is excellent for riding (not too hot and not too cold), the wind is only a light breeze, and there's hardly any traffic at all. It's the perfect antidote to the congestions of downtown Sturgis. One interesting thing is that, I swear, there is far more roadkill per mile in the Dakotas than any other place I've ever been.

I see a place called The Cow Town Mall. It's cute. I think of some malls I've been in that are the size of Rhode Island and here's this one, which has nothing more than a cafe, a post office, a Wells Fargo Bank branch, and a hair care place that also does nails. I walk into the Bull Creek cafe and enjoy an incredibly tasty late lunch of homemade roast beef, mashed potatoes and brown gravy.

Some time later, the air begins to feel a bit different and I know I'm close to water. Within minutes, I cross the Missouri River and ride into Pierre. There's something about the Missouri River that arouses a deep yearning in me, and whenever I hear it referred to as The Big Muddy, I go to a different place.

Within an hour I learn three things about Pierre. The first one begins with an apology to my kids. Remember when we used to drive to school and we'd practice memorizing the state capitals? Well, I misled you on the pronunciation of Pierre. It's pronounced PEER, not pee-AIR. It's true. I checked it out with every resident I met. I hope you'll forgive me.

The second thing I learn is courtesy of the night manager at the Burger King. Population-wise, Pierre is the second smallest state capitol; Montpelier, Vermont being the smallest. The third thing I find out is that none of the computer stores in Pierre sell Mac products. This is amazing. There actually exists a state capitol with no Mac stores. I ask the desk lady at my motel if she knows anyone who owns a Mac. She doesn't. Then I ask if anyone has an iPhone. She thinks of a few who might but doesn't know for sure. But at least she's heard of them.

So I get a bright idea and figure I'll go over to the Best Buy. They sell Mac stuff and they're everywhere, right? I check my iPhone and it turns out the closest Best Buy is in Bismarck, the capitol of *North* Dakota, over two hundred miles away. What a hoot! I have to ride a total of 385 miles just to power up my computer!

I usually don't have specific plans when I'm on a multi-day ride, but all along I had wanted to go into North Dakota for the simple reason that I'd never been there. In other words, riding up Highway 83 from Pierre to Bismarck fits perfectly into my plans. The almost-flat, grass-covered view doesn't change much except for some corn fields and these amazingly colored, expansive fields of sunflowers. And they're big sunflowers, too. Just sitting right there while their smiling and sun-tanned faces follow the sun as it arcs across the sky.

The kid at the Best Buy in Bismarck immediately finds the perfect power adaptor and I'm good to go. The following morning, I head west on Interstate 94. I originally had the idea of riding across Montana then down through the Yellowstone and Grand Teton national parks on my way to see the kids and kidlets in Colorado. But…. But then I see the sign for the Theodore Roosevelt National Park, home of the Badlands. The Badlands. *Bad Lands.* The name alone lures me away from my original idea of luxuriating in the lush Yellowstone and Tetons.

The entrance to the park is in the clean and western-proud town of Medora and there's a thirty-six-mile drive I decide to take. It's fabulous. The land itself is savage, broken and scabbed. Bold. But, like the desert, there's an at-a-distance beauty to it, a feverish unrest and recklessness. The only problem is getting a great photo. My small camera is a good one but it isn't equipped to capture the grandeur. Or maybe it's my lack of photographic skill. Or both, I don't know. Nevertheless, the ride itself is pure, worry-less joy. Until I turn a corner and twenty yards in front of me, ambling on and around the road, are about three dozen bison.

Now, I call my bike The Beast but these guys are a whole different magnitude of beast. They're big. And have big heads. And horns. And they can run up to 35 mph, which is damn fast for an animal that can weigh fifteen hundred pounds. The thing that worries me the most is that they're out here in the open with no supervision, which means they can do whatever they want wherever, whenever and to whomever they want, and I have no idea what they're thinking and planning. Plus, these are *Badlands* bison. Let's face it: fifteen hundred pounds at 35 mph can wreak a lot of havoc. Sure, my seven hundred pound beast can go more than three times faster but not on this road. And here I am, out in the open with no protection. May the Motorcycle Gods forgive me, but I think I'd rather be in a car. Better yet, a tank.

I turn off the engine and immediately think it's a mistake because when I start it up again, one of the big ones might take the unexpected roar of the engine as a challenge. I can see it now: The fifteen hundred pound group leader lining up in front of me, snorting and pawing the pavement, saying, "Okay Mr. Biker Human, game on. Let's see how badass that seven hundred pounder is!" Thankfully, however, they're quite docile and are not a problem. Nevertheless, I don't get too close. And that big one? He gives me the eye when I start up the engine so I quickly scoot on out of there and don't look back.

I spend the night in Glendive, Montana and the following morning ride eighty-some-odd miles to Miles City where I gas up at a convenience store. I want to get to Cheyenne, Wyoming via Gillette and want to make sure that the road I think is Highway 59 is, indeed, Highway 59. I walk in and see a sweet, elderly Montana lady wearing a dark brown straw hat with a dried yellow flower on it. There's a playful sparkle in her eyes.

Me: Hi!

Sweet, Elderly Montana Lady with a Sparkle and a Hat: Hello!

Me: Say, are you familiar with this area?

Sweet, Elderly Montana Lady with a Sparkle and a Hat: I am.

Me: Great! Is that Highway 59? *(I point)*

Sweet, Elderly Montana Lady with a Sparkle and a Hat: It is. Where are you headed?

Me: Well, I was thinking that if I went that way *(I point)* and I'm not too stupid, I'll end up in Gillette.

Sweet, Elderly Montana Lady with a Sparkle and a Hat: That's the way, alright. But don't worry, you can be a little stupid and still get there.

Weeks later, I recount the conversation to a good friend and he points out that the sweet Montana Lady came up with an excellent philosophy for life.

So I head on down the two-lane 59 on pace to make it to Cheyenne, Wyoming well before sunset. I come to some road construction and there's a twenty-minute wait for the pilot car. I'm off the bike, stretching the legs when a farmer steps out of the pickup behind me. He walks up and with no preamble at all asks, "So how'd ya like Sturgis?" Amazing! I'm three-plus days, three states and eight hundred miles removed from the rally and still there's the assumption that the only reason I'm here is because of Sturgis.

I'm back up to speed, 60-65 mph, and riding through the Thunder Basin National Grassland which, coincidentally, is covered with grass but, alas, I hear no thunder. About twenty-five miles north of Douglas, Wyoming I begin hearing a rapid boomp-boomp-boomp. My first thought is that it's the road, the surface of which is still a little rough. A few seconds later, my front end drops down about two inches and I'm riding on nothing but the front rim while the tire is wiggling all over the place. It feels like I'm riding a pogo stick on a rockslide. I'm slowly slowing down and praying that the white Acura behind me is doing the same.

I finally get to the shoulder and stop. When my heart rate dips below 150, I calmly take a full analysis of the situation and discover two things: I'm still upright and the front tire is, indeed, flat. I call for a tow truck and the sweet Wyoming lady tells me it'll be along in an hour or so. Ya gotta love it: I'm in the middle of miles and miles of nothing but miles and miles of prairie grass and no thunder, yet there are four bars on my cell phone, which is two more than I get in my own living room.

Twenty minutes later, two guys in a small white Chevy pull over and ask if I need help. (Of course, they're bikers.) I tell Glen and Mike about the tire and the tow truck and Glen says, "Have it towed to Vinni's – he'll do you right." He looks back at my bike. "Good thing you have a Harley and not a Honda or he'd probably be closed." I ask him for the phone number and address but he has neither. He says, "Don't worry. Everybody knows where Vinni's is." I thank the two good men and they take off. I get Vinni's number from 411 and he answers the phone.

Vinni: Are you the guy with a flat on the 59?

Me: Uh … yeah. How'd you know?

Vinni: Glen's wife called. What kind of bike is it?

Me: A Harley Deuce.

Vinni: Good thing. If it was a Honda, I'd probably be closed.

Me: Uh … of course! What's your address? I'll need to give it to the tow truck driver.

Vinni: Just tell him to take it to Vinni's; everybody knows where I am.

The tow truck shows up and I tell Houston, the nineteen-year-old driver, that I want to go to Vinni's but don't have the address. He says, "No problem, I know where it is."

We get to Vinni's, unload the bike and discover a deep, two-inch horizontal cut in the tire. It can't be fixed so Vinni sends his wife, Lindy, to I-don't-know-where to get a new one. I end up sitting around for an hour and a half talking with Vinni and his brother Bob in Vinni's personal bar, which is one half of the building right next to the shop. (The other half has three or four bikes in it.) What great guys! Vinni has a full beard and biker hair, wears an old t-shirt and old jeans, smokes a pipe and drinks rum and coke after rum and coke. And he has a Scottish accent. He's been to Sturgis thirty-five years in a row (thirty-five years!) and tells me all sorts of legendary stories, some of which I can't repeat in mixed company.

Lindy brings back the new tire, we go back over to the shop and Vinni gets on the floor to unscrew the Allen screws on the bottom of the forks. Then he does something impossible. Now, I don't know about you, but whenever I use an Allen wrench it takes me at least four tries to find the right size. But Vinni? He's down there on the floor, in the late afternoon shadows, looks for no more than a second or two and says, "Shit, it's metric! Bob, bring me a metric set." How can he do that? Not only does he know the right size, he knows it's metric just by looking at it for a second!

Vinni and Bob change my tire and even change my front brakes, which really needed changing. All for a real decent price, too. Tell ya what, my friends, if you're ever around Douglas, Wyoming needing some superior work done and want terrific company and conversation, go see Vinni (unless you're riding a Honda) and tell him I sent you. And don't worry about finding the place. Everybody really does know where Vinni's is.

9

CHEAP MOTELS

When you're out riding, things happen. If you keep at it, everything happens.

Some are wondrous, some dismaying; some are metaphysical, some mundane. Sometimes you're hungry, sometimes you eat too much. Sometimes you're unbearably hot, sometimes painfully cold. You lose things and get lost; you find things and find your way. You fall in love, you find things to despise. You bleed and you heal; you get sick, then you're invincible. The rains pelt, the snows blind, the winds make you helpless. You ride through gorgeous scenery and through desolate wastelands; all places are the way they're supposed to be and they're all perfect. It's life in microcosm: One month of riding equals two years of normal living.

It's mid-afternoon as I'm riding south on US Highway 71 on the Missouri side of its border with Kansas. The Beast is humming along like it's supposed to, the road is in great shape, and the traffic is sparse. The occasional rains, which are never hard or cold, give a richer hue to the grasses, bushes and trees that frame my route, left and right. Above, the bustling clouds wear halos of silver and gold, and there's always another brook or stream or river to cross over. (For me, riding over water has always been a special enjoyment.) It's nothing but a pleasant ride. Truly pleasant. It's so pleasant and problem-free that I untether my mind and let its thoughts mingle and wander according to their own inclinations. Eventually, I reflect on the different ways riding a motorcycle affect me.

I stop at a gas station in Rich Hill and a smiling fellow walks on over. He looks at my license plate and asks, "California?" "Yep," I say. And then he asks the question that bikers get asked more often than any other. "Bet your butt hurts, don't it?" I answer, "Damn right!" but honestly, that's not the truth. The truth is that my butt *never* hurts when I'm riding. Never. That is, until I'm ten miles from my next stop. Evidently, there's something about ten-miles-away that wakes up this Pavlovian Dog Gene I have. It's odd. I'll be riding along just as butt-comfy as can be, but as soon as I'm ten-miles-away, my butt starts screaming in agony like it's being ripped to shreds by a bloodthirsty Rottweiler. However, the moment I step off the bike, it's gone. Poof! Just like that. But hey, at least I'm not slobbering.

I'm still on the 71, somewhere between Lamar and Carthage, when I head down a side road. It's a farming area and the few houses are set way back. The road's surface is also in excellent shape and most of the time I have it to myself. I get to cross over two streams that are lined with drooping foliage, and there's a rejuvenating coziness as the sound of my engine reverberates among the moisture-laden trees.

I've long since been of the opinion that "home" is wherever you plant your boots. This is why, I suppose, I don't have an aversion to cheap motels. Same with sleeping on the ground. Sure, these places are far from luxurious (oftentimes they're downright neglected) but as soon as you take off your boots, you're "home" and it's all good. Occasionally, however, a night in a cheap motel will challenge your ability to relax.

I roll into Joplin and find a cheap motel where, I swear, a porn film is being made in the room above me. There's an occasional bump and mumble but that's not what's making it hard to get to sleep. What's making it hard to get to sleep turns out to be still yet another lesson about cheap motels: When a porn film is being made, every five minutes a guy will drive up in a pickup with the music blasting so loud you can't tell if it's a jackhammer or four pounds of TNT blowing up, and to make sure you're not startled, he'll shine his bright lights through your cheap curtains.

The following morning I head west on Interstate 44. As soon as I cross into Oklahoma, a different Pavlovian Dog Gene starts wagging its tail and I get an irrepressible urge to say things like "I reckon" and "Set a spell." (Fortunately, this one doesn't make me slobber, either.) So I go along with the urge and begin to practice a cowboy accent, which makes the miles and the clouds just gallop on by. After an hour, I'm sounding pretty authentic and thinking I'll switch out my helmet for a cowboy hat.

I stop for lunch in Tulsa, and the way the streets are configured, the easiest place to get to is McDonald's so that's where I go. Except for the manager, all the employees are teenagers and, dang, they are working hard. I'm impressed with their industry and their aspiration to make this McDonald's the best McDonald's anywhere. Washing the already clean windows, wiping off the already clean tables, mopping the already clean bathroom floors, filling up the already full bins of condiments. Oh, the looks of joy on their smiling faces!

There is, however, one small problem: No one is manning a cash register and taking orders so that by the time the manager comes by, a hungry mob has filled up half the place. But the hungry mob is a peaceful Oklahoma one so no one complains and the cheerful atmosphere remains unsullied. And why would anyone complain? We're all in beautiful Oklahoma saying things like "I reckon" and "Set a spell." The thing is, by the time I get my lunch, I could have been halfway to Dallas.

I head south on US Highway 75 and can't help but marvel at the beautiful countryside, which is groomed so well that a number of times it seems like I'm riding through a perfectly manicured greenhouse. It's as if all the trees and bushes have been meticulously placed in order to create the greatest aesthetic appeal, as if Mother Nature is showing us how pretty, pretty can be. And it seems like I never go more than a few miles without crossing over a river or a stream; rivers and streams that create paths from their own intuitions, intricate paths that frame the meticulous vegetation in ornate geometries.

I'm still practicing my cowboy accent, which is now so thick that even my thoughts have a drawl to them. I'm also still thinking about that cowboy hat and start to have an urge to get one of those enormous silver belt buckles, too. When I cross the border into Texas, a third Pavlovian Dog Gene jumps up and starts licking my face and I begin imagining circumstances where I can say things like "I'm fixin' to" and "Sheeit."

It's amazing. And unavoidable. And Pavlovian. And still slobber-less, thank goodness. But sheeit, it's Texas, y'all, and I'm fixin' to visit some family so I reckon I'll set a spell.

The good times in Dallas are non-stop. Alison and Steve, my niece and her music-wise hubby, offer up some fine Texas hospitality and take me to the Goodfriend Beer Garden. It's one of the better hamburger joints in the world, partly because the floor manager is the cutest, nicest, most efficient and most curvaceous redheads I've ever seen. I'm so taken that I don't care what I end up eating or what it tastes like. I open the menu and the first item I see is a Redneck Burger. I don't bother to read what makes a burger a Redneck Burger but order one anyway only because it's the first time I've even heard of a burger called Redneck. Besides, I don't want to waste time looking at a menu when I could be watching the redhead. If you're interested, a Redneck Burger is a hamburger with fried baloney on it. And maybe a few other things you don't want to think about. Nevertheless, it tastes real fine just like I imagine a Redneck Burger should, and I cheerfully washed it all down with a tall glass of Velvet Hammer Beer. The redhead keeps looking prettier and prettier.

A couple of days later it's time to continue riding south and I sadly leave the good conversations of Alison and Steve behind. I head through downtown Dallas and make my way through the Gordian Knot of streets and freeways where there are Texas-sized chuckholes alternating with Texas-sized mounds of dried cement. Even on the freeways. Now, I have to slow down but the cars, pickups and trucks? They don't bother slowing down at all. In fact, if you know Texas you know that no one ever slows down anywhere in that state. Unless they're on two wheels trying to avoid chuckholes and mounds of cement.

I make my way to US Highway 67, which is in excellent shape, and ride southwest through some Texas farm country. At Hico (HIGH-coh), I head south on US Highway 281 and take a few side roads, which are all in excellent shape as well. I spend the night in Lampasas where I find a place alongside the Lampasas River to take photos of an exceptional sunset, after which I have dinner at the Dairy Queen where the local high school girls' soccer team is celebrating a victory.

The following morning I continue south on the 281 to Marble Falls. The Marble Falls Bridge is at the far side of the town and crosses over the Colorado River, but it's not the same river that runs through the Grand

Canyon. This Colorado River, which never leaves the state of Texas, starts out a little southeast of Lamesa and 862 miles later dumps into the Gulf of New Mexico south of Bay City. After crossing the bridge, I check out the surrounding area and it's a bit startling. Right here, in the middle of all these sprawling Texas farms and ranches, is an active resort area where people are fishing and kayaking and paddle boarding. There are even palm trees.

A half hour later, I come to Johnson City, which was named after an ancestor of our 36th president, Lyndon Baines Johnson. I make a right on US Highway 290, then another right on Ranch Road 1, which runs alongside the Pedernales River on the other side of which is LBJ's Texas White House, which is so big the entirety of Johnson City could fit in the living room. I rest for a while and take some photos and think how nice it must be to have a big river in front of your house. Just think of the great fishing that's always within walking distance.

It's here that I should say something about these country roads in Texas. Though there are exceptions, those west of US Highway 281 are called Ranch-to-Market (RM) roads, those east of the 281 are called Farm-to-Market (FM) roads. All the ones I rode are in superior condition, have very little automobile traffic, and most of them have a speed limit of 75 mph, so you can roll on the throttle to your heart's content. (But be on the watch for wildlife, especially deer.) Though Texas is big, these roads crisscross over all of it, meaning you're never at a loss as to where to go for a remarkable ride.

In addition to the great riding, there's another reason I like Texas. It's a tough environment unfit for timid souls or timid sounds, and it accommodates the roar from The Beast better than any other area I've ever been in. Bold men and women have molded the surface, but underneath, and forever, the land is ultimately indomitable. Even the colors have an uncivilized tint to them; the greens slightly gray, the sky a steel-like blue. The land infects you with keen discovery; your breaths become full, your movements fluid, your senses electric.

Not far before Fredricksburg, I head south on RM 1376. I'm in the Texas Hill Country, which is also known as the Texas Wine Country, and it's so pretty here you can't go more than ten miles without stopping for photos. It's also home to more artists per capita than almost anywhere.

Really. The towns in this area probably have more art galleries than gas stations.

The 1376 has no twisties and only a few sweepers but it does go up and down a lot. When I come to the top of every hill, I roll hard on the throttle and a few times and The Beast and I come close to getting airborne. The reason I'm on the 1376 is that it leads to Boerne (BURR-nee), which is where my big sister lives.

I'm fully energized when I get to Boerne and even more so when I see my beautiful big sis, Jette, and her big-hearted Texan, Gammon. (Every time I see Gammon I always thinks how neat it must be to have an ancestor who rode with Teddy Roosevelt's Rough Riders.) Jette shows me her newer paintings and let me tell you something, my friends: She is one big sis who can flat out *paint*! For three days our conversations and laughter amble in concert with the friendly clouds in the Texas sky and there is never a moment of dissonance. Jette is also a terrific cook and the whole time I'm there, I wonder why Gammon doesn't weigh at least 400 pounds. I chuckle at the wide contrast between making a "home" for a night in a cheap motel and feeling at home with Jette and Gammon.

I get a late start and – y'know, just now as I write that, I realize that that's the phrase I use more often than any other. I get a late start. Must have written it a hundred times by now. And said it a thousand. I'm long overdue for a new expression and … lemme see …. Oh! Here's one I heard years ago. I take off at the crack o' noon.

Jette, Gammon and I keep finding things to talk and laugh about, so I end up leaving Boerne well past the crack o' noon, heading west on Interstate 10. I'm still in the Texas Hill Country so the views are nice, very nice, but as I go west, the hills deflate as the sun gets hotter. At Junction, I decide to see what San Angelo looks like and an old cowhand gives me directions: north on US Highway 83 then left on US Highway 87. When I get to San Angelo, the day is crispy hot and the hills are all but gone. I stay on the 87 a while longer, pass through Big Spring and end my ride for the day in Lamesa.

The following morning, I head straight west on US Highway 180. This area, which is in West Texas south of the Panhandle, is pretty much covered with farmland. The crops are planted quite a ways away from the road and I'm guessing the farmers did it like that because of a lack of water, though the people there are hesitant to use the word drought.

The mercury is rising up and up and the entire sky, and it's a *big* sky, is pure blue except for one small, white cloud, and I find myself hoping it'll float my way so I can enjoy its shadow for a few moments. At Seminole, just before the New Mexico border, there's a time and temperature sign that says it's 102 degrees. If there's a breeze, it's not anywhere close.

The quality of the roads in New Mexico isn't as good as it is in Texas, and the speed limits lower accordingly. In Texas, you'll see speed limits at 80 mph but in New Mexico they seldom get up to 65 mph. Another difference is that alongside the roads in Texas are what are called picnic areas, most of which have gazebos with shade and picnic tables underneath. Many even have bathrooms with running water. In eastern New Mexico, they're called rest areas, but they're nothing more than run-of-the-mill turnouts; no gazebos, no shade, no picnic tables. But at least they're paved and, hey, if you're lucky, there'll be a port-a-pottie or two.

In addition to being sizzling hot, this area (Eastern New Mexico) is covered with oil derricks and that, ahem, quaint smell of crude oil is pervasive. How many miles I go hoping for a breath of fresh air, I don't know. There are more clouds now and I occasionally, and happily, pass through a shadow. Though these respites are brief, I do appreciate them. The only diversion in this utterly unexciting area is playing tag-you're-it with the occasional dust devil.

In Hobbs, there's another time and temperature sign and it says it's now 108 degrees. Gads! No wonder most of the bikers are off the road and standing in the shade at gas stations drinking anything cold. The heat has been constantly harassing my faculties and even though I've shortened the distance between stops down to thirty-five to forty-five miles, I too have a need to drink anything cold. After cooling down a bit, I decide to push through with the hope of some relief in the mountains after Artesia. Before I get there, however, I get a speeding ticket in Hope.

I'm quite a ways outside of town when I slow down from 65 mph to 40 mph because that's what the speed limit signs say to do, even though there are no buildings and no signs of human activity. Cop #1 passes me going the other way then makes a U-turn and starts tailgating me.

This smells of a speed trap (a smell reminiscent of hot crude oil) and as a lone rider with an out-of-state license plate I'm a perfect candidate. After a mile or so, he passes me (on a right-hand turn, no less) and races into town. After I make that right turn, I see cop #2 pointing his speed gun at cop #1. Now I know I'm getting a ticket. When I pass cop #2, he's already put away the speed gun and is climbing into his 4X4. A half mile later he pulls me over and tells me he *has* to give me a ticket because he caught me doing 52 mph in a 40 mph zone.

Let's face it, there's nothing I can do about it. I'm alone in the under-populated scrublands of New Mexico and I'm not going to fight a $94 ticket in a small town that's a thousand miles from home. And Cop #2 knows it. The most irksome thing is having to listen to his lecture about how speeding on a motorcycle is dangerous, how he's just looking out for bikers and saving our lives. (He actually says that: I'm just trying to save your lives.) And all the while he's smiling. Finally, he sends me on my way and tells me to enjoy New Mexico.

A half hour later, it cools down a bit in the Lincoln National Forest, which gets up to almost 8,700 feet. It's a fun route and quite view-satisfying, and were I not so heat-beaten and cop-lectured I'd be able to enjoy it more. The original idea was to spend the night in Las Cruces but the heat has taken its toll and my ride for the day ends in Alamogordo. I go to sleep wondering how it came to be called that. *Gordo* is the Spanish word for "fat" so does the name really mean Fat Alamo?

After an excellent night's sleep (no porno films were being made), I actually get, ta da!, a somewhat early start and despite another day of temperatures over one hundred, make it into Arizona and all the way to Tucson. I find another cheap motel (under thirty dollars a night) and as I'm unpacking, I realize that I've become a world-class expert on cheap motels. I decide that when I get home I'm going to write a doctoral thesis on the subject based on the extensive list of statistics I've gathered over the years. Here are a few.

There's a 37% chance your first door key won't work.

There's a 37% chance your second door key won't work.

There's a 47% chance the microwave won't work.

There's a 47% chance there is no microwave.

There's a 42% chance you'll have to unplug the TV to use the only outlet that works.

There's a 99% chance your laptop adaptor isn't long enough to reach that outlet.

There's a 55% chance there will be an unfamiliar smell in your room.

There's a 26% chance you'll sleep, fully clothed, on top of the bed covers for health reasons.

There's a 78% chance one of the light switches will be behind a door.

There's a 5% chance one of your neighbors is selling drugs.

There's a 5% chance one of your neighbors is making a porno film.

There's a 99.99% chance those two neighbors are the same guy and he's not friendly.

There's a 0% chance someone will ask how you liked your room.

There's a 100% chance your cheap motel experience will be unique.

Last, I will expound on the ecological advantages of the WiFi signal being relayed by carrier pigeons. The most exciting thing, however, is that after my thesis gets published, I'll be able to sign my name as Dr. Kinn, ECM (Expert on Cheap Motels).

As I continue through Arizona, the temperature is still triple digits and I'm still stopping every thirty-five to forty-five miles. I'm keeping up with the water and the electrolytes and they're doing a decent job of keeping me upright. When the road starts going through the hills, the clean, blue sky in front of me is dotted with the prettiest white clouds. It reminds me of that famous painting by Magritte called "Castle of the Pyrenees," and I keep expecting to see an enormous rock floating in the air. (Maybe I'm not getting enough electrolytes after all.)

My last stop is at a cheap motel in Quartzsite, which is just east of the California border. I've no sooner gotten off the bike when a guy with two dogs quickly walks up and starts talking. Excitedly. He's wearing red tennis shoes, his frayed jeans go to just below his knees, his hair looks like he took a bath with an electric generator, and his eyes have this yeah-I-fried-my-brain-in-the-'70s look to them.

'70s Fried Brain Guy: Shit, man, gotta get the dogs in, man!
Me: Uh, okay.
'70s Fried Brain Guy: Shit, man, they can't get dirty, man!
Me: Uh, okay.
'70s Fried Brain Guy: Shit, man, I gotta catch that thing, man!

Me: Uh, okay.

'70s Fried Brain Guy: Shit, man, it's a big one, man!

Me: Uh, okay.

I look up and, sure enough, there's a hellacious dust storm coming from the west and it's a big one, man, totally blocking out the sunset. As I walk in with my stuff, he's running out to "catch" that dust storm like a kid in Disneyland seeing Mickey Mouse for the first time. After the storm has passed, he's covered with an inch of dirt and has a big brown smile on his face.

Me: Looks like you had fun.

'70s Fried Brain Guy: Shit, man, I love that shit, man!

As I said, cheap motels are a unique experience.

This is my last night on the road for this particular trip. Tomorrow, I'll pack up, load up and gas up for the last time. On nights like this, I'm given to sweet reminiscing. When we talk of our journeys, we often talk about the things we saw and the places we visited. Most of our photos are of those things, too, so I guess it's natural to do that. But it's the people you meet that make it most worth your while. In the past five weeks, I've had conversations with hundreds of people I'd never met before. Most shook my hand warmly, gave me a genuine smile, and they all wished me well, as I did them. And while it's true that "home" is wherever you plant your boots, the times that most warm our hearts, when we feel the most at ease, when we're most at home are when we're with our family and friends.

10

SAVING the WORLD

Go now and then for fresh life.
Go whether or not you have faith.
Go up and away for life; be fleet!
—John Muir

There is freedom in riding a motorcycle. We've all heard and said that, and it's true, but it's not completely true. The complete truth is that riding offers many freedoms, not just one.

Take laundry, for instance. If you're riding alone, it's pretty much optional. Honestly, there's no problem with wearing the same pair of socks four or five days in a row. Even a full week. Same with a t-shirt and a pair of underwear. And when they get dirty, you have the freedom to turn them inside-out like you did when you were a kid and trying to fool your mom into thinking you didn't get grass and mud stains on your brand new clothes. One exception to this is when you're sweating a lot and have a sensitive nose, in which case you'll end up changing every three days. However, if you're riding with a group, you might want to reduce it to two days. You know, show a little consideration for the other riders. Now, if you have a good woman for a passenger, definitely make that one day. And if you're really on top of things, you'll have a handy bag of quarters for the laundromat. (Originally, I wrote: Remember to pack a lot of quarters. Nothing impresses a good woman more than a big bag of quarters. But somehow that didn't sound right, so I changed it.)

Then there's Old School: nothing but the clothes you're wearing and a blanket. No quarters, no laundromat, no one to impress. And the blanket is optional.

For several reasons, this autumn trip to the Pacific Northwest was a maybe/maybe not proposition and the should-I/shouldn't-I argument raged between my ears for weeks. Finally, the wanderlust gods hold sway and off I go on Interstate 5 North. The thrill of being on the road catches me full throttle as I pass Red Bluff, where the I-5 is aptly called the Cascade Wonderland Highway. The road surface is excellent, the traffic is light, the temperature is in the high fifties, and there's a comforting canopy of billowing clouds, white and gray and charcoal.

I've said a number of times that I enjoy riding over bodies of water and north of Redding I get to do it in an extraordinary way. I come upon what looks like a sprawling lake then find out it's actually called the Pit River Arm. I'd make a joke on the name but I'm too busy enjoying the extraordinary sights: the charismatic shorelines, the morning mist creeping over the mountaintops, the occasional wink of phosphorescent blue sky peeking through the redwoods.

The redwoods in Northern California always get me thinking about the incomparable naturalist and mountaineer John Muir, even though he's probably more famous for his writings about the giant redwoods in the Sierra Nevada in Central California. (Of course, thinking about him now may also have something to do with the fact that the Muir Woods National Monument is in Northern California.) It's undeniably beautiful here: the zigzagging rivers and streams, the thick mantle of meadowgrass on the mountains and, of course, the incomparable redwoods themselves.

I pass Shasta Lake and occasionally see the streams that feed into it, which reminds me of a time I went river fishing with my dad and my brother. Within seconds of throwing out my first line, I caught an eleven-inch rainbow trout. Easily my best day with a rod and reel. It goes without saying that every locale is unique, but it's interesting how each one has some characteristic that reminds us of another place. It could be a smell or a type of bush or tree, or the way sounds reverberate, or the colors of the buildings, or even the curling of the wind. Perhaps it's Mother Nature's way of saying that, yes, every place is different but there *is* a connection, no place is entirely separate.

I'm thinking about the similarities, large and small, that places have with one another and remember an experiment I read about years ago. The researchers wanted to find out what external stimuli, if any, affect the content of our dreams. So they gathered together some holocaust survivors and right before bedtime got them into a conversation about the holocaust and showed them photos of its atrocities. Most of them, if not all, ended up having nightmares about the holocaust. The researchers thought this was a significant revelation. My thought was: Really? You were surprised? Also, you must admit, if you want to find out if what we look at and what we talk about affect the content of our dreams, then experimenting with Holocaust survivors is a rather heartless way to go about it. Instead, why not get epicures to talk about luscious desserts, or show athletes pictures of trophies and medals, or get children into a conversation about puppies and kittens?

Patches of blue sky become a constant when I arrive in Weed, which is about fifty miles south of the Oregon border. Weed is a town with a literate sense of humor. I know that because this is the first sign I see: WEED LIKE TO WELCOME YOU!

I decide to have a chiliburger for lunch and end up sitting across a wooden table from a friendly fellow named Bond, who's wearing a Los Angeles Dodgers baseball cap. Behind him, nailed to a wall, is poster from one of the Star Trek movies.

Bond and I have been chatting about this and that for a while when two cute young women sit next to us. They're eating salads and I can tell they're annoyed with Bond and me but can't figure out why. We try to be friendly, even manage to say a clever word now and again, but they want nothing to do with us. Bond asks how they like their salads. They give us contemptuous looks and one of them says, "We're *vegetarians*, what do you think? How do you like your murdered cow?"

After the cute vegetarians leave, I mention to Bond that I'm on my way to Oregon. He leans over and with serious concern whispers, "Ya hafta be careful in Oregon, y'know." I ask why and he says, "Oregon's weird. Just be careful. It's weird." I ask for some examples and he tells me about underground societies where you can bet on women wrestlers, an annual festival celebrating plankton (or is it sea horses?), and one day a year everyone walks backward. Other things, too, like people who sleep while hanging by their feet, homeowners who live outside while wild animals sleep inside their homes, and men and women who are celibate but walk around naked while watering their rose bushes which, if you think about it, is pretty risky. I don't know if the things Bond says are true but, in an odd way, I want to think they are.

I head north on US Highway 97, which has only two lanes but the speed limit is 65 mph and there's hardly ever a reason to go slower than that. Not only are the views and weather so different from where I live in Southern California, the people are of a calmer temper and the traffic flows with an unwound mindset. To my right, the mountains Shasta and Shastina are posing all proud and personable as they still wear some of last winter's snow. The temperature is now in the sixties, the sky is crisscrossed with translucent, white clouds, the reddish-brown soil is covered with golden grasses, the mountains are low and flowing, and the air has that bracing autumn snap to it. A day and locale tailor-made for cruising, and that's exactly what I enjoy as I ride to California's northern border.

Within minutes after crossing the border I learn one incontestable fact about Oregon: It is a *damn* pretty state. The carefree way the golden Sugar Maples and the vermillion Japanese Maples are splashed against the clustered Ponderosa and Lodgepole Pines makes me think Mother Nature designed this state on one of her more lighthearted days. Even the insects are taking care to avoid my small windshield as much as possible. It's easy to see why Oregon is often referred to as God's Country and I can't think of anyone who would argue it.

My first Oregon stop is for gas and a snack at the Pilot gas station in Klamath Falls. I'm filling my tank when a large woman wearing yellow spandex pants walks right up to me. It's then that I have my first conversation with an Oregonian.

Large Pilot Gas Station Lady in Yellow Spandex: They have any shocks this year?

Me: *(Having absolutely no idea what she's talking about)* Uh … y'know … I don't recall seeing any.

Large Pilot Gas Station Lady in Yellow Spandex: They never do. Don't know why.

Me: Yeah, me neither.

No matter how hard I try, I cannot fathom in the least what just happened, so I go inside and buy a SoBe Orange Cream drink (gawd those are good!) and a nutritious entree of nachos with extra cheese. The total is $8.00 and, whaddya know, that's exactly what I pay! No sales tax! I'm *really* liking Oregon now! After my meal, I continue on the 97, which follows the eastern shore of Upper Klamath Lake for a stretch. The day has warmed up a bit, there's a sweet breeze coming from the northwest, and I'm happily on my way to Crater Lake.

I make a left onto Highway 62 where I immediately encounter a scheduling problem. The pastoral countryside is so fetching that it's forcing me (yes, it's *forcing* me) to stop every couple of miles to take photos, and I begin to think that at this rate I ought to plan on making it to Crater Lake tomorrow. I keep going, though, and enter the Crater Lake National Park in mid-afternoon. It's getting cold but I don't mind. Beauty is always worth a little discomfort.

Crater Lake National Park is stunning. Munson Valley Road is well-maintained and swashbuckles its way through the mountains as lively as possible. In addition to the remarkable scenery, I notice something else. A total lack of guardrails. I don't know if this is a good thing or not but I do know it makes the remarkable scenery even more so, bigger and more primal. The canyons to my right are so close and so deep and so guardrail-less that I'm thinking there should be warning signs for anyone prone to vertigo: WARNING! VERTIGO HAZARDS ABOUND! Thankfully, I don't get vertigo so I ride along with full faith in my bike to keep me on the pavement; la-di-da, la-di-da, not a care, taking photo after photo.

I turn left at the stop sign and – BOOM! – there it is! Crater Lake! An eruption of blue. I nearly fall over and think I'm starting to get that vertigo I never get. I shakily make it to the first turnout, walk toward the lake then stop ten feet from the edge of the guardrail-less cliff, which is so vertical that you can't see where it ends. I'm nervous. Now I *know* I have the vertigo I never get. My legs are shaking and it feels like my boots can't get a grip in the sandy dirt. It's like walking downhill on a wet tightrope after three triple espressos, or playing Twister on a playground slide covered with ball bearings. I get visions of falling down the cliff and the little angel of safety in my head is telling me I should get back on my bike and back on the pavement where I'll no longer have that vertigo I never get. (Evidently, she has more faith in my tires than in my boots.) Instead, I slowly edge forward and brace myself against a tree so I can calm down and take in the view.

Commanding his domain on top of the world, Crater Lake sits in brooding blue and bold relief against an unsympathetic sky, the water like a solid, weighty mass anchored at the earth's core. The winds are unforgiving, the clouds hostile, the hidden shoreline mysterious, and I sense a calculating malevolence in the shadows below me, a malevolence who wants me gone. But there's a powerful draw from the dark blues and varied shades of gray, a color combination I have always found seductive. It's a magnetic pull, at once mesmerizing and freedom-giving. There's a lusty isolation to it that delineates your individuality, makes you bigger, more pure and invincible. I sit, harboring a push to go and a pull to stay, while the contrast of danger and beauty crackles through me like high voltage in a rainstorm.

When I leave, it's cold and dark and begins to rain so I get a room in Chemult, the first town I come to. The steak I have for dinner is decent but the huckleberry pie is the absolute best. My taste buds have never before experienced that marvelous blend of tart and sweet.

After dinner, I lie in bed thinking about my day, which was a good one. I think about the conversations I had, especially the one with Bond, and all the thoughts that had floated through my head. All the things I'd seen, too. Soon, the calming mountain air puts me into a deep sleep.

I roll into a town of about ten thousand and, to be honest, in the back of my mind I'm hoping to see one of those oddball Oregon sights. Fat chance. This place is about as wholesome as a family television show in the 1950s. So I'm riding along enjoying the wholesome sights on a wholesome Main Street in a wholesome town when I pass by something that makes me go, "Huh?"

I look in my rearview mirror and, sure enough, there's a cute and perky twenty-something woman walking down the sidewalk wearing nothing but a chastity belt. Naturally, I turn around. You know, I have

SAVING the WORLD

to make sure it's not an illusion. I pull up next to her, turn off the engine and say, "Uh, it's none of my business but I notice you're walking down a public sidewalk wearing nothing but a chastity belt." She defiantly walks up to me and with a spark of rage says, "Don't you know! We're saving the world!" She accents each word like it's an accusation, even stomps her foot a couple of times, her perkiness responding like perkiness does. Then she adds with a glare, "What are *you* doing about it?"

Honestly, I think to myself, I'm not doing anything to save the world, unless riding through the beautiful Oregon countryside will somehow make the Los Angeles Dodgers win the World Series. (As everyone knows, in any world that's been saved, the Dodgers always win the World Series.) The problem I'm having is not seeing the connection between saving the world and wearing nothing but a chastity belt, so the best answer I can manage is "Uhhh ... well ...." Her glare softens and she becomes overwrought. Tears are forming. "Why don't people understand?" she asks. I thoughtfully reply, "Uh, I don't know. I mean, you know, it's not easy." She looks at me a few moments like I might be one of the few who does understand. Then she gets this lost puppy look on her face. The corners of her mouth are drooping, she's staring at the ground and it looks like those tears might soon be running down her cheeks. I get a little sad, too, because it's not right that a cute and perky twenty-something woman who is saving the world is getting sad. "It's just so important," she says. "Yeah, it is," I agree.

She's sort of hopping around now so I look down and realize her feet are burning on the hot sidewalk. As my line of sight moves back up, I notice a heart-shaped opening in the middle of her chastity belt. Well whaddya know! The very item of interest it should be covering is right there, out in the open for everyone to see. It's then that I realize that in all these years I missed the irony. The "chastity" in chastity belt actually means the opposite of chaste. I think about it a few moments and figure out what must have happened. Centuries ago, when they first invented these things, they called them peek-a-boo belts but then figured they would cause a moral outrage so they called them chastity belts instead. You know, to fool the people who would get morally outraged. Excellent! I learned something! I feel smarter!

I also feel bad because her feet are still burning and she's still hopping around, so I offer her a ride to wherever she needs to be in order to save the world. She gratefully accepts my offer, I have her put on my helmet, she climbs aboard, and off we go. At the first stop sign, I look at our reflection in a store window and, sure enough, there's a cute and perky twenty-something woman sitting behind me wearing nothing but my helmet and a peek-a-boo chastity belt. It's not an illusion! It's a photo-op! Alas, no one is around with a camera.

After a couple of miles and a couple of turns, we come to the small park where the world will be saved. A healthy, middle-aged woman, who is also wearing nothing but a peek-a-boo chastity belt, walks up, hugs and kisses my friend on the cheeks and asks who I am. Athena, that's my friend's name, says that I stopped to help her. "Oh! You're here to help! How lovely! My name is Arsinoe." She shakes my hand. Vigorously. I notice two other things also shaking vigorously. I've come here to learn how the world will be saved but now my objectivity is clouding over. Smiling, Arsinoe steps between Athena and me and leads us by the hand to the exact place where the world will be saved. It's exciting. I never dreamed I would be part of something so important.

The park is surrounded on two sides with a thick pine forest; the ground is covered with thick, cool grass and dotted with clumps of trees and bushes. When we arrive at the exact area where the world will be saved, there are ten other peek-a-boo chastity belt ladies and a dozen men wearing nothing but speedo-type underwear. There's a long bench, a trailer, and a big iron pot sitting over glowing charcoal. Athena and I sit on the bench and Arsinoe announces to the peek-a-boo chastity belt ladies that I'm here to help. They gather around. I'm asked a lot of questions that test my sincerity to help but they're coming in so fast that I don't have time to answer any of them. Some of the ladies are skeptical, a few are even sneering.

Finally, one of the sneering ladies asks if I eat meat. Silence. Utter silence. They all stare. This is the big test, I know it. Somehow, I sense that eating meat is bad so I want to say I'm not a meat eater but then I'd be lying, and lying, especially about something that's obviously so important, might be against the rules of saving the world, which might stop the world from being saved and I don't want to be the cause of that. The solemn weight of responsibility descends upon me. The only thing to do, I realize, is to tell the truth and suffer the consequences. So I say,

"Well ... uh ... yeah." The sneering one who asked the question says, "I knew it!" and folds her arms and turns away. A few others turn away, too.

But Athena, Arsinoe and the others are more understanding. They begin to explain how saving the world works. I'm interested. I want to learn. I want to understand all of it so I can do my part without breaking any rules. It's a barrage of weighty philosophy and I'm doing my best to absorb it all but it's tough. In the end, this is what I am taught.

- Men are bad.
- Babies and animals are good.
- Meat is death.
- Vegetables are life.
- Peek-a-boo chastity belts make men start eating vegetables and stop killing babies and animals.
- Goodness will fall from the universe like invisible raindrops.
- The world will be saved.

Again I'm unable to see a connection, unable to grasp the logic. Maybe it's because I'm not yet spiritually aware enough and still have a lot to learn. (I am a man, after all.) Or maybe it's because it's hard to think clearly with twelve pairs of naked breasts staring at me. Or maybe it's because I eat meat. Whatever it is, I'm not getting it. Athena, Arsinoe and some of the others see my perplexity and take pity. Athena rests a hand on my shoulder and softly says, "I know, it's hard isn't it?" I nod. Arsinoe smiles in a motherly way and says I need a bowl of vegan soup to clean up my spiritual self.

Now, even though my knowledge of the subject is severely limited, I'm pretty sure vegan has something to do with vegetables, and vegetables, to be completely honest, scare me. Especially the green ones. So much so that in my whole life I've probably eaten no more than the equivalent of a medium-sized bowl of them. And then it was only under duress. I panic. I truly want to help save the world but do I really have to *eat vegetables*? It seems like an awfully extreme sacrifice. But then, I think, saving the world is important, right? I must think of the greater good, right? We all want goodness to fall from the universe like invisible raindrops, right? Suddenly, I'm filled with an awe-inspiring sense of duty and decide to accept the sacrifice of eating vegan soup.

The sneering lady who asked me about eating meat carries over a wooden bowl and a wooden spoon in the shape of a ladle. She antagonistically hands me the bowl and some of the soup spills on my pants. She glares, waiting for some sort of protest but instead I just thank her. I don't want to reproach someone who's saving the world and, besides, how can I get angry at a pair of naked breasts?

The soup is brown and in it are small, whitish cubes along with thick, light green leafy things. At the bottom are small variously shaped objects and in the middle is this long, round yellow thing that tapers at one end. I stare at it and experience something akin to the beginning of Armageddon. My sense of duty deflates, panic returns and I sit frozen, hoping for a miracle of deliverance, which happens when Arsinoe announces that it's time for "The Dance." I'm not expected to join in because, I figure, I'm not yet spiritually advanced enough. Besides, I haven't eaten my soup.

The twelve peek-a-boo chastity belt ladies form a circle. They dance one way, then the other and alternately reach up to the sky with open hands, then down to the ground. All the while they're humming and chanting. To my left, the men are holding hands and also dancing in a circle, and they've all taken off their underwear. Now this is one thing I can understand because being surrounded by all those naked breasts and peek-a-boo chastity belts has caused me to think about taking off all my clothes a number of times. But if I did take off my clothes, I'd probably have to join the circle of hand-holding men and I'm not too keen on that. So I sit, fully clothed, and watch the two Saving-the-World Dances. It's inspiring. I think I'm learning things. I think I'm getting more wise. But then, after a while, the weight of the bowl and the responsibility it represents commands my attention.

Again I look into the bowl of vegan soup. I wonder if it would be acceptable to sip some of the liquid and ignore the solid parts. I could maybe do that. But there are so many rules about saving the world that I don't know and I don't want to break any of them. And what would happen if I did break a rule, even one I didn't know about? Would it stop the world from being saved? I want to ask Athena or Arsinoe but they're in a circle, dancing and chanting. I sit, confused and worried, and wish I knew more than I do. Regrettably, the only safe thing to do is eat all of it.

I look at the solid parts more closely. I don't know what any of them are, except for a few things that look like kernels of corn. I know what corn is, of course, and peas and carrots, too. And sometimes I'll get a cheeseburger with lettuce and tomato on it, but tomatoes are actually a fruit so they don't count. The thing that worries me the most is the long, round yellow thing in the middle. I recall once hearing someone say the word okra and at the time it sounded like she was referring to a vegetable, so maybe that long, round yellow thing is an okra. But what if it's not? What if it's an alien life form? And say I nudge it with the wooden spoon and it gets angry and jumps up my nose and crawls into my head and starts eating my brain like in that Star Trek movie? What'll I do then?

I look up and the naked men are now standing around and watching the ladies. A few are excited. The ladies are still dancing but all their peek-a-boo chastity belts are in a pile in the middle of their circle. Now I'm really confused. How are they going to save the world without wearing their peek-a-boo chastity belts? Boy, I have a lot to learn.

I look at my bowl of vegan soup again then put it aside. Maybe if I sit still for a while the power of the Saving-the-World Dance will infuse me with enough lasting courage to finally eat some of it. Maybe even a solid part or two. And maybe the power will be so strong that I'll be able to nudge that alien okra thing and it won't eat my brain. So I sit still for a while and watch. Everything's fine. Wonderful even. I'm feeling the power of the Saving-the-World Dance wash over me like invisible raindrops of goodness. I think.

Then something alarming happens: The police show up. The tranquility and joy of the ceremony are shattered. The men quickly put on their underwear and even pants, shirts and sandals. The ladies quickly put their peek-a-boo chastity belts in the trailer and they get dressed as well. Then all of them stand with their hands behind their backs and wait for the handcuffs. I'm pretty sure this isn't part of saving the world but maybe, I hope, enough of the ceremony transpired that the world will be saved anyway.

But what if it didn't? What if all that's needed is a few more minutes of dancing and chanting? We're so, so close to saving the world! Again, I am panic-stricken. Some sort of action must be taken and it's up to me, and only me, to take charge because everyone else is getting handcuffed. Maybe, just maybe, I can do something to make up for my failure to eat my soup. Like stopping this intrusion of police. I confidently stride over to the officer in charge, a woman with a bored look on her face.

Me: They're saving the world, you know.

Bored Policewoman: *(Sighs)* Yeah, I know. They do it every year.
Me: Oh.

Later that night, after eating a double chili cheeseburger and feeling guilty about it, I check the news on my laptop and it's immediately clear that world hasn't been saved because the Dodgers lost in extra innings and are now eight games behind first place. Resigned to living in an unsaved world, I think about all I learned. I still don't understand any of it but figure that if I think hard enough and long enough, some gems of wisdom will come to me. So I think and think and think some more. I don't come upon any wisdom but there are two things I'm pretty sure of, two things needed to save the world, and I hope that some day all people everywhere will know and apply them.

1. Someone has to eat vegan soup.
2. Ladies, start wearing nothing but peek-a-boo chastity belts!

The following day I continue north on the 97 through the Deschutes National Forest. It's a fact that national forests are gorgeous and Deschutes is no exception. But then, I think, every bit of Oregon I've seen is as gorgeous as a national forest. In La Pine I come upon a gas station that sells ethanol-free gas, which is something I'm interested in, so I try it out. Turns out that my engine loves it – The Beast sounds more contented and beefy – and so do I because it gives me an extra three to four miles per gallon.

It's time for an oil change so I go to the Wild Horse Harley dealership in Bend, where the wall of the lunchroom is covered with Harley t-shirts from all over, including one from Tikrit, Iraq. Imagine, a Harley dealership in Iraq! When it comes time to pay for my oil change and a t-shirt that says "Rally Bound, Hammer Down," my debit card is rejected. This is embarrassing. I call the bank and the crisp and proper bank guy informs me that their system was compromised (gotta love the euphemism) and my debit card number may have been stolen. But not to worry, I'll get a replacement card in two or three days.

Well, that's not going to work. I'm more than a thousand miles from home, have no more than forty bucks in my pocket, and I'm pretty sure that Wild Horse Harley wants to be paid for the oil change and that t-shirt. (I'm a no-credit-card guy.) The bank guy says I can go to a bank branch and get a temporary card. That won't work either because it's Saturday afternoon and the banks are all closed. They're closed tomorrow, too, because it's Sunday. I tell him I'm headed east so he says I can get the temporary card in Boise. That's fine, but Boise is over three hundred miles away, forty bucks won't get me there, and I can't get my bike until I pay Wild Horse Harley. I need some help here! Finally, he authorizes the oil change and t-shirt purchase, then gives me a half hour to get to an ATM to get enough cash to get to Boise. I make it with two minutes to spare.

The next day I head east on US Highway 20 through southeastern Oregon, which is like a different state. To the left and right, the low mountains are sparsely covered with shrubs, bushes, and short trees. The shade is sparse as well but the temperature is in the sixties so it's not a concern. Highway 20 parallels the Malheur (MAL-yer) River for much of the way and I pass by an occasional corn-growing farm and an occasional ranch where contented cattle graze on grass, which is their preferred cuisine. I stop for gas and a snack in Vale, on the outskirts of which is the Bates Motel. Alas, I forget to go back and get a photo.

Right before the Idaho border, I stop for another short rest in Ontario and meet another biker. His grizzled hair is gnarled, his goatee is curled up from the wind, and his Harley Road King has seen a lot of miles. He has weighty personal matters on his mind and his monologue is non-stop. He lives in Wyoming and is on his way home from San Francisco after visiting his ex-girlfriend from twenty-some-odd years ago. He had had so much to tell her, so much to get off his chest, but could never bring himself to open up. The whole visit was awkward. Finally, as he sat on his bike ready to leave, he managed to blurt out that he still loved her and always would. She just shook her head and walked away. My friends, there is a beautiful, tragic sweetness to a big, strong, tattoo-covered biker gazing into the distant west with tears in his eyes.

11

MUSIC

Whatever deceptions life may have in store for you,
Music itself is not going to let you down.

—Virgil Thompson

Riding out of the Denver, Colorado area on my way to New Mexico, I take Interstate 76 to Interstate 70 to Highway 470 to US Highway 285. I'm in the Pike National Forest where the sky is huge. (It has to be to hold all these mountains.) At the beginning, the Rockies are somewhat conservative in appearance, by Colorado standards only, but as I go higher, they become like giant spires of iron that dare the imagination.

It's late in the summer and the weather could not be better. Right before Pine Junction, I catch my first glimpse of the mind-boggling colors of the changing Aspens – yellow and maroon and every hue in between – decorating the forever-green pines. After Pine Junction I take a left onto Pine Valley Road and at Buffalo Creek I take the right fork onto Deckers Road, which crosses over the South Platte River and leads to the mountain community of Deckers. At Deckers, on the corner of Highway 67, sits the mountain equivalent of a strip mall, which means it's a strip mall with personality.

But something's amiss. Despite scenery to die for, perfect weather and riding a bike I love, my enthusiasm level has been going lower and lower. I meander around a bit, eventually get a lemonade and slump into a wooden bench on the wooden veranda under a wooden overhang and have a chat with Bruce, a fully-bearded local resident wearing denim overalls. Bruce is loudly reprimanding bikers who complain about all the sand and gravel on Deckers Road. "If'n they don't like sand 'n' gravel s'much, they c'n just stay outta the mountains!", he bellows. "Hell, sand 'n' gravel'r part-a the mountains bein' mountains!" He glares at me and lowers his voice to a grumble. "It is, y'know." In a way, I like Bruce. He is what he is and that's that.

I take Highway 67 south and ride by Westcreek, which has a population of only a little over a hundred. I don't actually see it because most of the buildings are on the other side of the hill to my right. The only reason I know it's there is because I saw it on a map before I took off in the morning. The odd thing is that I don't feel adventurous enough to ride over there and check it out.

About twenty minutes later I roll into Woodland Park, a pretty town where there is a lot of building construction going on. It's easy to see why the town growing. It sits between eight and nine thousand feet amid pines and aspens, the air is healthy, and it has outstanding views all around. Despite those outstanding views, I stand outside a convenience store and do nothing but stand there. For some reason the views are not inspiring me the way they normally would; in fact, they're hardly affecting me at all.

From Woodland Park, I take US Highway 24 heading west. I take it all in and, despite the Colorado Rockies being an endowment from paradise, maybe paradise itself, I'm still weighted with the doldrums. Ahead on the left is the famous Pike's Peak, still wearing a cap of snow on its famous peak. The 24 goes through the southern end of the Pike National Forest, flattens out for a while then, at the San Isabel National Forest, it merges with US Highway 285, which I take south. I'm back on the 285.

To my right are four of the famous Fourteeners. Fourteeners, as any Coloradan will eagerly tell you, are mountains with an elevation over 14,000 feet. Colorado has a total of fifty-three of them, including Pike's Peak and the ones to my right: Mt. Princeton, Mt. Antero, Tabeguache Peak, and Mt. Shavano. I don't know that I could point out those four Fourteeners, I don't know if what I'm looking at are actually those four Fourteeners, but I do know they're there. Coloradans are proud of their fifty-three Fourteeners, as well they should be. They're a brotherhood of grandeur. But to the proud Coloradans, there is one source of irritation concerning the Fourteeners and it has to do with my home state, California.

California has only twelve Fourteeners, no irritation there. The irritation is that one of them, Mt. Whitney, is the highest mountain in the continental United States, a mere seventy-two feet higher than the highest mountain in Colorado, Mt. Elbert. Now, I like Mt. Whitney. Not only was it the name of my high school, but you can hike (*hike*, not climb) to the summit from the west side and on the way up you have what might be the best view you'll ever have of the giant redwoods. But it's not that big of a deal to Californians that Mt. Whitney is in California. In fact, I'd bet that most Californians don't even know that a mountain called Whitney exists, much less that it's the highest mountain in the continental United States.

I'm filling my tank in Pine Junction when a guy driving a pickup starts a conversation. He finds out I'm a Californian and immediately says, "Y'know, Colorado has fifty-three Fourteeners, more than any other state! Nanner-nanner, we win." (He doesn't say the nanner-nanner part but it *is* implied.) I smile. I'm happy for him, I really am. Nevertheless, he looks at me like he's itching to get into some sort of highest mountain verses Fourteeners argument, but I don't want to do that. Instead, I say, "Really? Colorado has fifty-three Fourteeners? Wow! That's amazing!" But he's not mollified and keeps looking at me with eyes that say, "Don't you dare mention Mt. Whitney!" So I don't mention Mt. Whitney, but I can tell that he just doesn't want to let it go.

Looking at those four Fourteeners off the 285, or looking at what I think are the four Fourteeners, gets me thinking. Mt. Whitney is listed at 14,505 feet. As a kid, I distinctly remember reading it was 14,595 feet. What happened to those ninety feet of mountain? The only explanation I can come up with is that there's a secret society in Colorado, the Very Secret Coloradan Fourteener Society, and they sneak over to California when no one's looking, probably at night, with these giant diamond-studded files and they've been filing off Mt. Whitney's summit for years. Their vision is that someday Mt. Whitney will be the second tallest mountain in the continental United States. Keep at it, fellas, only seventy-three more feet to go!

My enthusiasms have all but vanished when I arrive in Salida (suh-LIE-duh) via Highway 291. Salida is wedged between the San Isabel National Forest, the Great Sand Dunes National Park, and the Rio Grande National Forest, but the Salida area itself is pretty level, and that's where I decide to spend the night. I arrive on the north side of town a half hour before sunset, which looks like it'll be a gorgeous one. I want to find some lodging before the actual sunset comes so I can photograph it, but I spot only two motels. One has no vacancy and the other is no longer a motel but some sort of public housing.

It's odd. Salida is at the junction of two fairly well traveled thoroughfares (Highways 291 and 50) so there must be a lot of motels, despite a population of under six thousand. I ride back and forth on the five or six downtown streets a few times but I don't see any other motels. That's not to say there aren't any because, still feeling dull and uninspired, I'm mostly just staring straight ahead. Whatever the reason, I decide the best thing to do is ask someone in a convenience store.

The young, pretty woman at the convenience store assures me there are many, many motels in Salida. I say that this seems odd because I've been riding around and around for a while and it seems to be the one thing *missing* in Salida. (I don't mention feeling dull and uninspired.) I also mention I came in from the north and she asks if I tried the south side of town.

This is one of those awkward moments when you realize you didn't do the obvious. (Why does this only happen when I'm talking with a pretty woman?) I try to come up with a mature response but all I can manage is, "Oh...well...uh-huh." She smiles and suggests I go three blocks that way. (She points.) So I go three blocks that way and, whaddya know!, there's Highway 50 and it's covered with motels!

It's sad. The sinewy electricity that usually buzzes between me and The Beast has deteriorated to something along the lines of the "thrill" of riding up and down the escalator at Macy's on Christmas Eve. I miss photographing a spectacular sunset by twenty minutes and my cheap motel room turns out to be pretty high-priced despite the single-ply toilet paper. Even my favorite dinner, an eight-piece bucket of chicken-only and a two-liter bottle of Squirt, doesn't cheer me up. I try to figure out what's wrong but come up with nothing. Zero, zilch. Nada, nil. The big ol' diddly-squat. I go to sleep wondering.

My plan is to leave early and get in a hard day of riding, but that "something amiss" thing is still with me when I wake up. I mosey on down to the motel office (yes, I remembered to dress first) to get my free breakfast, which turns out to be watered-down orange juice and a Van de Kamp's pastry. I pass on both. I walk back to my room, hungry, thinking about this "something amiss" thing, when out of the proverbial blue it comes to me. I haven't listened, *really listened*, to any music for almost a month!

I eat the only thing remaining from last night's feast (a cold chicken wing), lie on the bed for I-don't-know-how-long and listen. Just listen. The laptop's speakers are small (no low end) and don't get very loud but, hey, it's music! And whaddya know, that "something amiss" thing has finally gone a-missing! I listen to Beethoven's *Opus 59* and the sheer genius, the undeniable energy, the unassailable mastery, make my heart pound and yearn for all things great. Dream Theater's *Constant Motion* blows me away. *Ramblin' Man* (The Allman Brothers) makes me want to live on the road forever. A big smile crosses my face when I hear Willie Nelson sing one of the greatest traveling songs ever written: *On the Road Again*. Here're the tracks from my playlist, which I had set to play in random order.

GLI UCCELLI — RESPHIGI

CONSTANT MOTION — DREAM THEATER

HOUNDS OF ANUBIS — WORD ALIVE

SAILING SHIPS — WHITESNAKE

FANTASY — EARTH, WIND & FIRE

OPUS 59, NO 3 — BEETHOVEN

DARK ETERNAL NIGHT — DREAM THEATER

BLACK WIDOW OF LA PORTE — JOHN 5

BEAT IT — MICHAEL JACKSON

DESPERADO — THE EAGLES

ON THE ROAD AGAIN — WILLIE NELSON

SING THE WIND FANTASTIC — MIKKELSEN

I WANNA DO BAD THINGS WITH YOU — JACE EVERETT

If This is It — Huey Lewis & The News
Take it Easy — The Eagles
Lyin' Eyes — The Eagles
Lookin' Out My Back Door — Creedence
String Quartet #15 — Mozart
Ramblin' Man — Allman Brothers

I get a late start but don't care. I alter an old biker proverb to suit my own philosophy, such as it is: You *can* outrun your destiny on the open road and you *can* choose the road. The electricity between me and The Beast is back and buzzing, the air is crisp, the sky is blue, the aspens beckon and the winding roads are daring me. Before you can say, "Which way to Santa Fe," I'm caught up in the verve of a devil-may-care ride.

And what a ride it is! I'm back on the 285 south of Poncha Springs when I pass by a copse of aspens huddled closely together right next to the road. I photograph them from several angles, look at the mountains and the sky and turn around and ride those last ten miles again. The way it's all configured makes me feel like I'm doing 500 mph.

I stop for lunch in Saguache (suh-WATCH), a nice quiet town with a library in the park, for a slice of pizza and a root beer. (Some day I'll get into vegetables, I promise myself.) Next is Alamosa and that's where you notice that you're leaving Colorado. Right around here, the cosmopolitan/cowboy ambience of Colorado begins to give way to the shadowy mysteries of New Mexico. I go into an old grocery store to buy some beef jerky and a little dog with a wagging tail closely follows me all the while.

Later, I gas up in Antonito, which is right on the southern border. At first glance there's nothing remarkable to it, but if you look, really look, you'll soon discover that someone, or several someones, have put forth a lot effort to make Antonito unique. There are fabulous murals on the sides of buildings and grain towers, and there's an old train depot with a small water tower, on the side of which is hand-painted "Cumbres & Toltec." On the side of one building is a round mural of two fish, not identical, arranged in a yin-and-yang design. I stand there a while wondering what the implication is.

While riding, I think about music, how it affects us and why. Music is a communication, we all agree on that, and it's interesting to compare it to spoken and written communications. Words have definitions and without those definitions, we could say something as simple as "Pass the salt, please" and never get any salt. The reason spoken and written languages work is that the individual elements, the words, have meanings. "Salt" has a meaning (several, actually) and it exists independently from the sentence "Pass the salt, please." It's the same with all the other words.

But it's not like that with music. Even though music is a way to communicate, not one element of it has a definition. What's the sound of a trumpet mean? Nothing. What's the meaning of a particular rhythm? Nothing. What's the meaning of a minor chord? Nothing. True, when we listen to a piece of music, we often attach meanings to it, and sometimes composers attach or add meanings, but the point is that none of the building blocks themselves has a meaning. Music is a universe-wide communication without meaning. This is what Stravinsky alluded to when he said, "Music means nothing but itself."

Then there's the element of time; that is, time in the everyday sense. To varying degrees, we're all subject to it, even those of us who don't wear watches. Check out time is 11 A.M., microwave for eight to nine minutes, take your vitamins once a day, the baby's due on March 17th. Time is pervasive, even if you try to avoid it. Our everyday lives are a sequence and coincidence of events, and we measure them with seconds, minutes, hours and so on. Music is also a sequence and coincidence of events, so there's a similarity. In music, however, time is measured in beats, measures, sections and so on, and those things are not based on everyday time. Indeed, they actually *create a different time*, a different world. The result is that when you listen to music, you step away from everyday life and the pervasive burden of seconds, minutes and hours, and into another world where seconds and minutes and hours have no relevance. Freedom!

I'm still on the 285 when I cross into New Mexico. It begins to rain, the wind kicks up several notches and it's getting colder. Up ahead I see blue sky and figure I'll brave the elements because it can't be that long before I'm in sunshine again. To my right is the gently sloping San Antonio

Mountain. Still, the rains come harder, the winds kick up even more, and the temperature plummets, so I decide it's time for the chaps and the jacket so I pull over and pull on the warm leather. As I'm zipping up I notice a car about fifty yards in front of me also pulled over. A barefoot girl in short blue shorts and a white tank top has gotten out and is taking pictures. I look to the east to see what so interesting and, my oh my, there it is. New Mexico has blessed my visit with a double rainbow!

I continue south on the 285 and before Santa Fe, I see a road sign that says Las Vegas is one hundred miles away, and for a few moments it's disorienting. (Turns out there *is* a Las Vegas, New Mexico and it's the Las Vegas where Doc Holliday lived for a couple of years beginning in 1879.) I check into a quaint motel in Santa Fe. In the bathroom is a photo of Annie Oakley along with one of her quotes.

Any woman who does not thoroughly enjoy
Tramping across the country on a clear, frosty morning
With a good gun and a pair of dogs
Does not know how to enjoy life.

New Mexico is a grand irony. Countless unique rock sculptures, impossible-to-describe colored soil, and clouds and skies that couldn't belong anywhere else. All of these impressive physical phenomena, yet by far the biggest impression is a metaphysical one. It's as if the whole state is angled a bit off from everywhere else so you keep thinking nothing's quite right when it actually is. I'm convinced that everyone who lives there knows what's going on and, in a magical way, knows exactly where you need to be, and it simply takes a little time for us visitors to catch up. The best way to understand how this works is to try this experiment:

Go to Santa Fe. As soon as you get there, you'll be lost (trust me) and there's no way to find your way in the usual way because there are so few traffic signs showing you the way. (You gotta hand it to the city and state governments for saving all that money by not putting up a lot of traffic signs. Merchants, too, for not spending money on those silly address numbers for their shops.) Anyway, keep going on whatever street you're on and the traffic will be such that you can't change lanes. Pretty soon, however, there'll be a break in traffic close to an intersection and you'll think, "Okay, what the heck, I'll turn here." A couple of minutes later, sure as shootin', you'll be where you want to be. It's magic! So the lesson is when you're traveling in New Mexico and you can't change lanes because of that guy in the pickup next to you, take the hint and don't turn until he lets you over.

The next morning I ride southwest on Interstate 25. I pull over on the far side of Albuquerque (a name that's much too hard to spell) and listen to a phone message from Mindy. She says she found my wallet on a street corner in downtown Santa Fe and she's leaving it at the reception desk in the Hotel La Fonda. I check my jacket and my bag and, sure enough, my wallet's missing. I call Mindy-the-Angel and thank her and offer to paint her house for free because she's an angel for returning my wallet. She laughs and says it's not necessary, which is good because I don't know the first thing about painting houses, and she wishes me a safe journey. (She gets it!) I ride eighty-five miles back to Santa Fe, get lost, turn at an okay-what-the-heck-I'll-turn-here intersection and a couple of minutes later I'm at Hotel La Fonda, which is at the end of the original Santa Fe trail. (I know that because it says so on a rock in the park across the street.)

Downtown Santa Fe is an up-scale place with a southwestern charm. Mostly adobe one- and two-story buildings, narrow cobblestone streets, lots of one-of-a-kind shops, and one-way streets. The guys in the parking lot let me park for free in a no parking zone. (They get it, too!) I'm tired, sweaty and unkempt but walk through the front doors anyway, only to find that the Hotel La Fonda is a pretty foo-foo affair, in a southwestern type of way, of course, but nobody stares or sneers or holds their nose when I walk by. A bunch of people even smile. Or maybe they're laughing at me, I'm too tired to tell which it is. The guy at the reception desk is cordial and cracks a joke. Before giving me my wallet, he says, "I'll need to see some ID first." I ride back to Albuquerque and spend the night.

The next morning I backtrack a bit on the I-25 then head northwest on US Highway 550. As I'm riding into Bernalillo I come across another off-angle oddity. On the northeast side of town is a sign that says Cuba (that's Cuba, New Mexico, not Cuba the country) is sixty miles away. A couple of miles later, on the northwest side of town, there's a sign that says Cuba (the town, not the country) is still sixty miles away. Evidently, there's some sort of time/mileage warp in Bernalillo but never mind. I get to Cuba (the town) and everything is just peachy.

I'm thinking of spending the night in Farmington and I'm pretty sure I'm on the right route but want to be certain so walk into a convenience store and ask the guy behind the counter. Immediately, the guy in line behind me, tall and hard-built, starts giving me down-to-the-tenth-of-a-mile directions. I'm impressed. He knows every side road, farmhouse and jackrabbit between Cuba and Farmington. Later, while outside, he asks me why I'm going to Farmington. I tell him it's because I saw it on the map, which is true, that's the only reason.

Out of the blue, he gets incredibly angry and starts yelling. "There's no good reason to go to fuckin' Farmington! It's a fuckin' shit hole. Why do you wanna go to a fuckin' shit hole?" I shrug my shoulders and calmly repeat that I saw it on a map. He glares at me. I'm thinking, he's younger, bigger, stronger and faster than me and it would be a good idea if I left. When he walks around to the other side of his van, still yelling invectives about Farmington, that's exactly what I do.

At a casual glance, the countryside is unremarkable scrublands. Though invisible, one thing that is remarkable, however, is that pervasive and mysterious, off-angle feeling. Another is that the elevation is around seven thousand feet, which, to me anyway, seems like an awfully high elevation for scrublands. However, the truly remarkable, almost shocking, sights are these grand, solitary, nature-made rock sculptures hundreds of feet high; some gray and white, some adobe-colored, the rest dark brown. There is a savage splendor about them. Each sits alone, a cathedral separated by miles from the others. Timeless. Millennia of wind and rain have cut deep geometries into the faces so that each has its own human-like visage, a priest of his own parish of bush and soil.

I spend my last night in New Mexico in Farmington, which, despite the lacerating vehemence of the fellow in Cuba, is a quiet and industrious place. I ride around and even walk for a while on the sidewalk next to the Animas River. Because the 45,000 people living there are spread out over a large area, there's a definite small town feel.

After dinner, I lie on my bed and think about music. If it weren't for music, I would still be in a funk and could not have enjoyed the magic of New Mexico. When I was in my twenties, I took to figuring out the magic of music. Why, I wondered, is music so coveted by everyone? Basically, all it is, is sound; ordered sound, yes, but its basic form is sound, which is nothing more than the movement of air molecules. It's not even the molecules themselves. To put it another way, music has no mass or matter. But therein, I determined, is the magic. Music is most like a spirit in that it's not made of "stuff" and, as such, it's the most spiritual of all art forms. All other art forms have some sort of "stuff" as part of them. Paintings have paint and a canvas, photos have photographic paper, dance has bodies, film has a screen, books have paper, and so on. But in it's basic sense, in it's basic manifestation, music is motion. Much like riding a motorcycle.

12

O CANADA!

The marvelous views, grand and minute, never end and all you have to do is look. Just engage in the simple, effortless act of looking. When you do that, only that, you see magic, sights you never imagined, and you realize again how utterly fine this world is.

Canada. That's where I want to go. I confidently roll out of Billings, Montana, going northeast on Interstate 94 and I'm on my way there. I'm excited. As far as I can see, the land is either flat or slightly sloped and it's all covered with yellow grasses. The effect is that you feel unrestricted, like you could take off in any direction at any time and there's nothing that could stop you. I call it the Montana I-can-do-anything attitude.

My first stop is to gas up in Forsyth. Forsyth is in two distinct sections, with the residents and their places of business on the north side of Main Street and the travelers' places on the south side. I accidentally find myself on the resident side and ride around. The two most notable places I see are the large Howdy Hotel (love the name) and The Roxy, a movie theater that, according to the sign on the side of the building, proudly opened its doors in 1930. (And I thought the Roxy in Hollywood was the original. Hah!) It's a neat little town and it reminds me of what Visalia, my own hometown, looked like when my age was still single digits. I feel at home and I like it.

I continue on Interstate 94 past Miles City and up to Glendive, where the I-94 starts going east. However, I continue on Highway 16 northeast to Sidney and northwest afterward. My plan is to cross into Canada at Regway, but the reason I chose Regway is because of a Montana town twenty-five miles before the border called Plentywood. I'm curious to see if the town looks like its name. I get to Plentywood and, not surprisingly, there are more trees than what I've already seen in this part of Montana, but it's nowhere near the forest I was halfway expecting. I ride around for a while and it, too, is a neat little town and it also reminds me of years-ago Visalia.

The 16 is going straight north now but a little past Raymond I run into a problem, and it's a sizable one. Road construction. Serious road construction. Were I a little more commonsense-minded, I would head back to Raymond and take a different route. There's even a sign saying the road is unsuitable for motorcycles, but I've adopted that Montana I-can-do-anything attitude and decide to keep on going. Besides, this is the shortest route and Canada isn't that far away.

At serious road construction sites like this, you have to follow a pilot car (some places call it a guide car) which is a good idea because there's no pavement, meaning no actual road, and there are a lot of large trucks constantly speeding around, some of them spraying water. While waiting for the pilot car I have a chat with the woman holding the stop sign. (Another clue that it's serious road construction is when there's someone holding a stop sign.) I tell her I want to get into Canada as soon as possible. She looks me up and down and gives me a little encouragement. "You can make it," she says, "just keep on going." The guide car turns out to be a heavy-duty pickup, which is to my advantage because by staying in the ruts created by its back tires, I negotiate that three-mile stretch of wet sand without a problem.

However, at the second stop, the stop-sign guy tells me that there are some places where there's nothing but mud one to three feet deep. That doesn't sound like much fun – maybe for a dirt bike but I'm on a seven hundred pound cruiser – so I take the only other road available, which is called 9 Mile Road and it leads west. (I so much want to keep going north into Canada – it's so close! – but what other option do I have?) Coincidentally, 9 Mile Road ends after nine miles and I have to go south on a road that evidently doesn't have a name. That's right, I'm now actually heading *away* from Canada on a road with no name. I pass by a place called Outlook, which, even for a Montana town in the countryside, must be small because all I see of it is a sign that says Outlook. Just after that sign, I head west on Soo Line Road, which dead-ends at Daleview Road where I head south again. South again? Will I ever make it into Canada?

These are country roads. And I mean *real* country roads. You know you're on a *real* country road when it's not much wider than a pickup and the biggest impression you get is an utter lack of population. Or you check your odometer, figure you have about sixty miles left in the tank and worry that it's not enough. I'm still going south on Daleview Road when I pass by the Big Muddy Golf Club (I see the sign but not the club) and wonder if the number of members is single- or double-digit. Going north into Canada is becoming more improbable by the minute so now I'm beginning to think that going south to Mexico would be easier and faster. Eventually I get to Highway 5 at Redstone, which, from the looks of it, has more metal silos than people. But at least it has a street called Main. I go west on Highway 5 past Flaxville and stop in Scobey. I check my map and, Aha!, there's a border checkpoint only fifteen miles north of me! How'd that happen? I'll finally make it into Canada!

The road is Highway 13 and I wonder if it's bad luck and I'll run into more road construction and end up having to head south to Mexico again. Thankfully, Highway 13 is not bad luck and there's no wet sand or deep mud, and it keeps going straight north. It doesn't take long and (trumpet fanfare) there it is! Canada! I joyously roll into the checkpoint at Coronach, which is manned by one (count 'em, 1) border guard. But hey, he's Canadian! And his Canadian Border Guard uniform is clean and perfectly ironed. And he has excellent Canadian posture. He comes out and meets me with an unimpressed look on his face.

Me: Wow! That's Canada! *(I point)*

Canadian Border Guard with Excellent Posture: *(Still looking unimpressed)* May I see your license, please?

Me: Sure! Say, it must be great living in Canada!

Canadian Border Guard with Excellent Posture: *(Still unimpressed)* May I see your passport, please?

Me: Sure! Being Canadian must be a lot of fun!

Canadian Border Guard with Excellent Posture: *(Still unimpressed)* Do you have any weapons?

Me: No. Well, I have a little Swiss Army Knife on my keychain. *(I show him. He's still unimpressed.)*

Canadian Border Guard with Excellent Posture: Wait here, please.

He takes my license and passport inside the border checkpoint building to check me out and I'm curious if the jaywalking ticket I got in college will show up. I get out my camera, stand in the doorway and ask if I can take some photos. He tells me to please wait outside but, yes, I can take photos but not of the American side. I wonder what would happen if I did take photos of the American side but figure that whatever it is, it wouldn't be pleasant (post 9-11 jitters and all that), so I take photos of only the Canadian side. He comes back outside and hands me my driver's license and passport. He's rather cheerful now so I ask him if my jaywalking ticket showed up. He smiles and says it didn't but several speeding tickets did, and he advises me that the Canadian police are strict about speed limits.

Me: So if I get caught doing ninety miles-per-hour in a ninety kilometers-per-hour zone, and I tell the policeman I'm sorry but I'm an American and just got mixed up with the miles/kilometer thing, do you think it'll stop him from giving me a ticket?

Canadian Border Guard with Excellent Posture: *(Smiling bigger now)* Mmm … no.

Me: Oh.

I tell him I want to get to Highway 6 and he gives me concise directions but they're so different from what I'm used to. "Go that way (he points) about fifteen or twenty minutes and turn right. You'll know where because it's the only place with brown cows. Well, most of them are black but there are a few brown ones. I think the house is blue but it's set back from the road and you might not see it." And it goes on and on from there. There's no way I can remember all of it, or hardly any of it, to be honest, but I don't tell him that. Instead, I thank him and figure I'll get directions along the way. Finally! Yes! I roll into Saskatchewan, Canada!

Hour 1: I practice spelling Saskatchewan.

Hour 2: Having gotten lost while practicing how to spell Saskatchewan, I try to find out where I am.

Hour 3: The national anthem seems appropriate so I sing "O Canada" over and over at the top of my lungs. It's a good thing no one can hear me for two reasons: I can't sing and the only two words I know are "O" and "Canada."

O Can-a-da

O Can-a-da-uh-uh

Hour 4: I try and find a town with a population higher than twelve.

You know how you hear all the time about how nice Canadians are? Well, it's true. Courteous drivers who *never* drive above the speed limit, pleasantly lilting voices, trashcans alongside the highways, you get your gas *before* you pay for it (the trust!), and their dollar coin is called a Loonie. How can you not love 'em? For a long while I try to figure out why Canada is so happy and finally come up with the only possible answer. Canada must not have any crime or criminals. What else could it be?

Canada offers a fun, while-away-the-hours thing to do while riding: converting kilometers to miles. Once, I get mixed up and go from miles to kilometers instead of vice versa and find myself almost out of gas. Converting liters to gallons would while away some hours, too, but instead I ponder two unanswerable questions. 1) What is the kilometer equivalent of the word mileage? Kilometerage?; and 2) How can a country this big have no criminals?

Another interesting thing. When you ask Canadians how far away something is, they'll always tell you in minutes or hours, never kilometers or miles. They'll say something like, "Ooh, I don't know, it's about three hours." (Maybe they're mixed up with the kilometers-to-miles thing as well.) Also, I did meet a few who pronounced "about" as "aboot," which is happily charming. It's like a cousin to the route/rowt-route/root thing in the United States.

Saskatchewan strikes me as one really big, really prosperous farm. Rolling hills that stretch forever, mellow black cows congregated around sparkling blue ponds, grasshoppers with colorful wings like butterflies and really big flying bugs that really hurt when they smash into your shins. The roads are in okay shape, mostly straight and rather narrow, but it's not a problem because there's hardly any traffic at all.

Still lost, I see a sign for a town called Big Beaver. Well, this is a place I have to visit so I ride into town expecting to see ... well, *something*. I park in front of the general store. No one's there. I look around and, sure enough, the place is deserted. In the whole town, there is absolutely no one. Not even a big beaver. Except for this friendly elderly lady in an old, dirty, beat up Chevy whose daughter lives in Long Beach, California. It's a bit odd; a friendly elderly lady in an old, dirty, beat up Chevy staring at me as I look around and see no one else. She watches me for a few minutes then drives over.

Friendly, Elderly Big Beaver Lady: The store's closed afternoons.

Me: Okay. Can you tell me how to get to Highway 6?

Friendly, Elderly Big Beaver Lady: Ooh … Do you know which way it is?

Me: *(Pondering the irony)* Well, I'm pretty sure it's somewhere over that way. *(I point)*

Friendly, Elderly Big Beaver Lady: Ooh…*(She looks one way, then the other)*

Me: I came from that direction. *(I point again)*

Friendly, Elderly Big Beaver Lady: *(Excited now)* Ooh … Well, go back out to the main road and keep going the way you were going but *stay on the roads with asphalt.* Don't go on the roads that don't have asphalt or you'll get lost. Just stay on the asphalt and you'll find it.

Me: Great! Thanks!

Friendly, Elderly Big Beaver Lady: Stay on the asphalt!

So I go out, turn left, stay on the asphalt for a while and eventually pull into a place called Co-Op in a town called Bengough (BEN-gawf). Turns out the Big Beaver Lady's directions were excellent.

My ultimate destination isn't Highway 6, however, it's what Highway 6 leads to, which is the city of Regina, the capital of Saskatchewan. Now, as an American, I look at the word Regina and naturally pronounce it "ruh-JEE-nuh." Well, it turns out Canadians pronounce it "ruh-JIE-nuh," which rhymes with that female body part called the Vag…, oh never mind.

So here I am at the Co-Op in Bengough and I can't figure out how to get the gas pump unhitched. I'm looking at it, helpless, when a young and very pretty Canadian girl comes out to help. She slides a card and, voilá, the gas pump is mine to manage. Now, at the time I don't know the Canadian pronunciation of Regina, which rhymes with, well, you know.

Me: Say, do you know how to get to Highway 6?

Young, Very Pretty Canadian Girl: *(Bright, innocent smile)* Oh! You wanna get to ruh-JIE-nuh?

Me: *(Staring, mouth slightly open, thinking she said "You wanna get to my Vag...?," but finally gathering a bit of composure)* Uh, don't you mean ruh-JEE-nuh?

Young, Very Pretty Canadian Girl: *(Still smiling but her eyes are saying: Ha! Flustered another American!)* Oh, in Canada we pronounce it ruh-JIE-nuh.

Me: *(Somewhat relieved but a little disappointed)* Aha!

I get my gas, park my bike, and walk into the store. The young Canadian girl is behind the counter with her friend, another young and very pretty Canadian girl, and I can tell they've been snickering about yours truly, the flustered American. I smile, chuckle and nod (it *was* a pretty good schtick) then commence strolling up and down the aisles expecting to find the typical mini-market fare. Instead, I find shelf after shelf filled with nothing but farming, hunting and fishing gear. I wonder what patrons in Los Angeles would think if they walked into a convenience store and saw the shelves stocked like this. I find the half-aisle with edible items on it so I get two staples of a wholesome diet: beef jerky and a Fanta Orange soda.

As I walk outside, a local biker pulls up. We chat for a while and he tells me I'm only thirty-five to forty minutes from Highway 6. Good news! And he gives me directions: Go that way (he points) about ten to fifteen minutes and turn right and you'll come to Highway 6 about twenty-five to thirty minutes later; turn left and about an hour later you'll be in Regina. I want to say something witty about the Canadian pronunciation of Regina, but I guess I'm still a bit flustered because I come up with nothing. He tells me to be safe and rides off. I leave as well and follow his directions: ten to fifteen minutes turn right, twenty-five to thirty minutes turn left, and just as he predicted, and hour or so later I'm in Regina eating a corn dog.

After spending the night in Regina, I ride east into Manitoba on Trans-Canada Highway 1 (TCH 1) and it's not long before I make the obvious observation that it's accurately named. It *is* a highway and *not* a freeway. It has two lanes either way and the traffic never gets thick but you do have to stay alert for crossing traffic. (Those big trucks take off slowly.) The longer I ride the more hilly it becomes. There are more trees and shrubs, too. And the sky! The cloud scattered sky stretches in all directions to all points infinite. Looking around at all this natural wealth, I decide to take some side roads.

Even though I'm never far from some sort of civilization, there's a homestyle alone-ness to it all. I wonder what it would be like to live there. I often do that when riding. I look at people eating and traveling and walking to and from their homes and cars, and wonder what their lives are like. I want to know them. Heck, I want to know everyone everywhere. I want to know what colors their walls are painted and why they chose those colors, what their silverware looks like, what knick-knacks decorate their shelves. But more than that, I want to know what it's like to *be* them. What are their worries, their hopes, what makes them smile.

About thirty miles west of Portage la Prairie, I pull into a little settlement called Sidney and wonder if there's a relationship to the Sidney in Montana. I slowly ride up and down the streets: Oak, Cypress, Maple, Elm, Poplar and South Railway. I smile and nod to some local folks and again wonder what it's like to live there. Sidney is a small place and it's not fifteen minutes before I've ridden along every street and end up facing TCH 1. To get back on the highway, I have two choices. I can turn left and backtrack a quarter mile, which, for some silly reason, seems terribly inefficient, or I can turn right and hope to find another entrance. I turn right.

The road soon turns to gravel and I'm about to turn back when I see a sign for the Shady Oaks Campground. Hmmm. I ride another hundred or so yards (or should I say sixty or so meters?), and there it is: The Shady Oaks Campground, home of MOBS, the Manitoba Old-Tyme and Bluegrass Society. There are still a few hours of sunlight left but this seems like an ideal place to spend the night.

The competent lady who owns the place and competently runs the very small store, tells me where the nicer campsites are. I didn't pack a tent so I ask her about the mosquitos.

Competent Lady Who Owns the Place: *(Smiling confidently)* Ooh, we don't have mosquitos here.

Me: Uh, are you sure? I've never slept in a campsite without mosquitos.

Competent Lady Who Owns the Place: *(Still smiling confidently)* Ooh, I'm sure. We have no mosquitos.

Me: That's a startling fact. Are you really sure? I mean, mosquitos are everywhere.

Competent Lady Who Owns the Place: *(Chuckling)* Been here fifteen years and never seen a one.

Me: I don't know what to say. This must be a magical place.

Competent Lady Who Owns the Place: Well, Mr. Kinn, I don't know about that but if you get bit by a mosquito tonight, I'll refund your money.

Me: Excellent! I love guarantees!

On my way to one of the choice campsites, I pause to look at the other campers, most of whom have mobile homes the size of intergalactic spaceships. They're enjoying their covered verandas and reclining chairs and card tables and electricity and running water and bathrooms and kitchens and TVs and computers and cell phones and beer. I have a bike and a sleeping bag. I would like to camp next to them, drink a few brews and chat and get to know them, but tonight I want the coziness of being alone. I make my temporary home in the southeastern-most corner where I'm out of sight from everyone else. As the crickets begin their nightly chorus, a train rumbles by a hundred yards away and I can feel its weight.

I sit under a three-quarters moon and eat my dinner: cold beef stew out of the can and potato chips. I crawl into my sleeping bag next to The Beast, rest my head on my leather jacket and begin again, amid the chorusing crickets, to think about my fellow inhabitants here on earth. Mothers reading to their daughters, fathers wrestling with their sons, old lovers walking slowly, young lovers who run. I'll never get to know all of them and it is a regret. Sometime in the night, I'm awakened by another train passing by.

Three things change as you go east in Canada. There are more trees, more lakes, and more signs in French, which isn't a problem at all because, hey, I've read the backs of more than a few bottles of shampoo in my life. *Sud* = South. See? It's easy! Once you enter Ontario, TCH 1 becomes Trans-Canada Highway 17. I don't know the reason for the change of numbers and neither does anyone I ask, so it must be another one of those unanswerable questions like why there are no criminals in Canada. So I'm rolling along on TCH 17 and feel like I've entered a photographer's paradise. A naturalist's paradise, too. And a hiker's and a fisherman's and a hunter's. Actually, it›s a paradise for anyone. Every time you turn a corner there's either a lush meadow surrounded by trees or a dark blue, crystalline lake surrounded by trees. It's so picturesque that the hardest thing to do would be to take a bad photo.

I'm so caught up in the beauty of it all that I get worried that it'll end after the next turn. But it doesn't end. I take every side road available around Clearwater Bay and Keewatin (there aren't that many) and I never see anything remotely dull.

Toward the end of the day, I get a comfy motel room in Kenora. After spending last night in a campground, I'm so excited about the luxury of a bed and hot and cold running water that I decide to do my laundry. Another thing I do is check my map and it turns out that most of the lakes in Ontario don't have names attached to them, which isn't surprising because with so many of them, they must have run out of names long before they were half done.

The next day, I continue east on TCH 17. One of the unnamed lakes I come to has an old, partially rusted, white railroad bridge next to it and I think it'd make for a great photo, especially when the sunset arrives. I walk across TCH 17 and see a sign that says Sunshine Lake. So it does have a name after all. But for some reason the name never made it onto the map. I begin to suspect that all the lakes *do* have names, but I wonder why they aren't written on the maps.

I think what must have happened is that after carefully placing a couple of dozen names of lakes on their maps, the mapmakers got tired of the detail and precision it demands and decided instead to pull out the Jack Daniels and the Southern Comfort and have themselves a riotous party. I can see it now. Mapmakers, each with a bottle in hand, dancing between their computers on top of map-making tables singing along with Johnny Cash, "I've been everywhere, man, I've been everywhere." You can hardly blame them. Writing a skillion names on a skillion lakes would be unbearably tedious.

I take at least a hundred photos of and around Sunshine Lake, trying all sorts of different locations and angles, but I never get that I'm-getting-great-photos feeling. I'm certainly not getting the feeling when a nondescript sunset shows up. At first it's like thousands of other nondescript sunsets but I take some photos anyway then head back to TCH 17, walk across it, and over to where my bike sits.

I take some photos of a large, dead, brownish-orange dragonfly that had gotten squished between my cables. (It may take a biker to truly appreciate this.) I see a hand-painted sign that says "Free Kittens" and I take some photos of that. My attention had been on only my immediate surroundings for a good ten to fifteen minutes when I sigh deeply about not getting a great sunset photo and decide to continue my ride. But just before I mount up, I see something that almost knocks me over.

It's a sunset. A glorious sunset. A gloriously spectacular sunset. A sunset that had exploded into view while I wasn't paying attention. A sunset so much more vast than any other I'd ever seen. The incandescent yellows and oranges and blues and purples stretch all the way across the sky, from farthest west to farthest east, farthest south to farthest north. I am filled with wonder. I take more photos. And more photos. And more photos still. I want the earth to stop spinning and rotating so the sky will remain like it is, so that I can stand in this three-dimensional "photograph" for the rest of my life.

Alas, the earth continues to spin and rotate and soon that vast, glorious view fades to dark. A nipping cold quickly moves in and it's time to go. I button up, zip up, and fire up The Beast and merge onto TCH 17 toward Thunder Bay.

Thunder Bay. I was a kid studying geography when I first came across the name Thunder Bay. Wow, I thought, what a great name! I wanted to go there immediately simply because of the name, but never did until tonight, this night of the vast and glorious sunset. There were several other places that also caught my fancy when I was a kid. Something about their names aroused a yearning, a wanderlust, in me and I wanted to visit them, too. The Himalayas, New Zealand, Yarlung Tsampo, The Strait of Magellan, Nome, The Aegean Sea, and a half dozen others. Some day, I promise myself, I'll visit all those places, too.

I wake up the following morning, ride around and just love Thunder Bay. I make my way down to South Water Street where there's a small, well-trimmed park with a perfect view of the Sleeping Giant, which is a peninsula that juts into Lake Superior. When I was a kid, the name Sleeping Giant made Thunder Bay even more exotic and here I am finally looking at it in person.

I continue northeast and eventually end up back on TCH 17. I'm trying to find my way to the Sleeping Giant Park but don't see any signs, so when I come to Ontario Road 587 I stop at a place called Can-Op and ask for directions. The fellow stares quizzically at me several moments before he says, "Ooh, you're right where you want to be!"

So I head on up the two-lane 587, a living, green oasis that's lined with thriving grasses and trees and bushes with small, grayish-blue flowers. The road itself is in darn good shape and gives me intermittent but darn good views of Lake Superior, but the thing that impresses me the most is all the dazzling colors of green.

At Pickerel Lake, I stop to stretch my legs and eat some trail mix. It occurs to me that Pickerel Lake, and all the other lakes in the Sleeping Giant, are sitting inside of Lake Superior, which means they're lakes within a lake. It's like Mother Nature's version of a swimming pool on one of those huge ocean-going cruise ships. For a long time I'm deluged with the infinite blues of the lake and the sky and the infinite greens of the trees and grasses. I wonder why it is that when it comes to clothes, the combination of blue and green together seem unnatural and I usually don't like it, but in nature it's splendidly aesthetic.

Early that evening, I get back to my room and think: I finally made it to Thunder Bay and the Sleeping Giant! So I go all out and celebrate with a nutritious, gourmet meal: an eight-piece bucket of chicken-only and a two-liter bottle of Squirt. I'm content. It's my last night in Canada so I sing myself to sleep with the national anthem.

O Can-a-da

O Can-a-da-uh-uh

O Can-a-da-uh-uh-uh-uhh-uhh-uhhhhhh

13

MIDDLE HEART

It is the music that makes it what it is;
It is the music which changes the place
From the rear room of the saloon in back of the yards
To a fairy place, a wonderland, a little corner
In the high mansions of the sky.

—Upton Sinclair

First, a word about Kansas. Ever since I was a kid, before I knew what Kansas was, all I've heard about it (other than from the Wizard of Oz) was that it was flatter than a pancake. Well, maybe I'm riding in the non-pancake part of Kansas (there are mounds as high as twelve feet!), but what I see isn't much different from the undulating, grass-swept lands of Eastern Colorado. Or Nebraska or Iowa. Or parts of the Dakotas and Montana and Wyoming. And I never heard anyone say those states were flatter than a pancake. Why does Kansas get singled out like this? It's unfair. I could maybe agree that it's flatter than a Belgian waffle or a strawberry blintz with whipped cream, but not a pancake. (And I don't mean one of those cheap blintzes with strawberry preserves; I want the *real* thing with *real* strawberries and *real* cream that's actually whipped.) Allow me to simply state the truth and you may quote me: Every pancake I've ever seen was flatter than Kansas. Every one. In fact, we who know the *real* Kansas should join together on a crusade. The next time you see a pancake, shout out, "Woah! It's flatter than Kansas!"

There are three straight weeks of riding a mostly circuitous route behind me and I've finally come to within twenty-four hours of one of the most exciting places anywhere. I'm experiencing the kind of giddiness you felt when you were a kid and went somewhere or did something new. Like in third grade when you went on a field trip to the local bakery. Or when your dad bought you your very first banana split. Or the first time you went to YMCA camp. It's *that* exciting! Anyway, this is it. Located a little north of Lebanon, Kansas is the traditional geographical center of the forty-eight contiguous states; latitude 39° 50', longitude 98° 35'. C'mon admit it, you want to be there!

Before I go any further, we should all salute geography masters Hagadorn and Beardslee, the two guys who figured it out back in 1941 when there were only forty-eight states. They must have gone through a lot of trouble. Especially when you consider that they did it all with nothing but slide rulers and the ability and patience to do long division by hand. And not make a mistake.

I'm riding east on Interstate 70 through Eastern Colorado. There's a nonchalant breeze but the exact moment I cross the border into Kansas, just like that, it turns into a gale force headwind that hits me in the face like a big sack of pancakes. Or Belgian waffles. It's so strong I feel like a bobble-head doll on the back of a MotoCross bike. Thankfully, it's back to a nonchalant breeze in twenty minutes and I can enjoy the non-pancake sights.

I look to my right and see a wide rainbow falling out of the clouds about thirty miles away. It starts to sprinkle but the sky above me is pure blue; there's not one cloud, not even a puffy white one, for miles. How does that happen? Then I learn that Kansas is the home to the biggest groundhog in the world. I know it's true because I read it on a sign. Twice. It's also home to the world's largest ball of twine. Saw that on a sign, too.

Ten minutes later, the winds pick up again and they never, ever stop, all throughout Kansas. I had wanted to get all the way to Norton but all that wind has tired me out so I decide to spend the night in Colby. The first two motels I go to have no vacancies, so I ride into downtown, which has streets of red brick. I see a guy parking his bicycle in front of Mabel's Cafe and Lounge, so I ride on over. It's here that I learn an important lesson about traveling: Never try to get directions from a guy standing next to a bicycle in front of a bar.

Me: Say, do you know if there's a cheap motel around?

Colby Guy with a Bicycle: Uhhhhhhhhh ... yeah. Didja go to Sturgis?

Me: Sure did! Do you know where that motel is?

Colby Guy with a Bicycle: Uhhhhhhhhh ... Hey, where ya from?

Me: Southern California. So do you know where it is?

Colby Guy with a Bicycle: I think it's over that way. *(He points)* Didja go to Sturgis?

Me: Uh, yeah. Do you know what street it's on?

Colby Guy with a Bicycle: Uhhhhhhhhh ... Hey, where ya from?

Me: *(slowly being beaten into submission)* Uh ... you know ... around.

And on and on it goes.

I finally extricate myself from circular-minded Colby Guy and head back out to Interstate 70 where I find my first Motel 6 where the WiFi is free.

The following morning, I'm so eager to get to Lebanon that I take off without eating breakfast, going northeast on US Highway 83, figuring I'll find a cafe or convenience store after getting in some miles. There are a bunch of towns within ten or so miles of each other so it's not going to be a problem, right? I pass through Roxford and see nothing. Not even any people except for a guy sleeping in his car in the city park. Same with Selden but, hey, it's the home of the 1991 world champion livestock auctioneer, Colonel Roger Emigh. (Another sign.)

I'm really hungry now and fantasizing about pancakes and Belgian waffles so when I get to Dresden, I actually ride up and down the streets

– there's got to be at least a grocery store – but I see nothing there either. And still no people. I ride around Jennings and it's the same except for a beer bar but, alas, there are no beer nuts. However, I do appreciate the fact that these places are clean and quaint, with wood-paneled houses, potted plants and porch swings. But by now my stomach is growling louder than my engine.

I ride around Clayton and see a guy sawing wood – a person! – and ask him where there might be some food. He thinks (yes, he *thinks*) the closest place is in Norton, which is twenty miles away. As my stomach begins to eat itself, I finally realize that these aren't towns at all; they're just neighborhoods and everyone is inside either sewing quilts or writing doctoral theses on desert survival techniques of the ancient Macedonian army. With shoulders slumped, I know I have no choice but to ride those twenty miles to Norton. But then, I think, that prairie grass is starting to look mighty tasty.

I get to Norton and, my gosh, there are people! Dozens of them! Walking around tipping their hats and saying, "How ya doin'?" There's a McDonald's, a Taco Bell, a Dairy Queen, a couple of convenience stores, and a theater showing an R-rated movie! Opulence! Elation! I feel like I just dropped into downtown Manhattan on New Years Eve! I buy one of those already wrapped-up cheeseburgers that convenience stores keep warm in glass cases and, well, it's probably a little better than prairie grass. I also stock up with trail mix, beef jerky and water.

I head east on US Highway 36 toward Lebanon and have only seventy-five miles to go. As each mile passes under my boots, the excitement grows and grows and the landscape gets greener and greener. Even the cows are getting happier. Soon, I'll be in the exact center, the nucleus, the hub, the core, the nexus of … of … the Nexus of the Middle! Can there be anything better? I'm smiling. Teeth showing. What a glorious day!

The happy miles keep zipping under my boots and right when my smile can't get any bigger, I come to US Highway 281, turn left and there it is in all its splendor: Lebanon, Kansas, population 217 and a gas station. A mile later, I turn left on KS 191 and a half mile after that I finally arrive at the world famous Nexus of the Middle. What a sight! A small patch of grass – lawn grass, not prairie grass (it's a good thing I'm not hungry any more) – a small chapel, a gazebo with picnic tables under it and, ta-da!, the seven-foot-high monument itself! There's a flag pole on it, on which is the Kansas state flag and above that is Old Glory herself, waving in the Kansas wind like she's saying "Howdy" to the world.

No one else is there and there's no parking lot so I set The Beast on the grass right next to the monument. I take a bunch of photos then watch a guy in a white Pontiac drive up. It's Marshall from New York, a caregiver for his ninety-year-old grandmother, and he's on his way to Denver to hang with some college chums from the '70s. It's interesting. He's a stranger from the east coast, I'm a stranger from the west coast, and here we are meeting at the Nexus of the Middle.

Marshall and I chat a while, shake paws, wish each other well, and he leaves. Fifteen minutes later a black Chevy 4X4 with a camper starts circling the place. The two guys inside are checking me out. Closely. After ten minutes of circling I guess they figure I'm not a maniac with grenades and an AK47, so they park the truck in the middle of the side road then walk on over. It's Mike and Paul. They're local residents, two of the 217, who've come out to the Nexus of the Middle to sit on the bench, drink a 12-pack of Keystone Light, and chat with yours truly for a couple of hours.

It's the best! Tell ya what, Mike, in his suspenders and white straw Stetson hat, is a walking, talking, beer-drinking encyclopedia. He informs me that almost all the state highways and roads in Kansas go either straight east/west or straight north/south. Then he covers everything from conversations between Andrew Carnegie and Abraham Lincoln to Bruce Springsteen's *real* (and somewhat sinister) roots to the cloning of George Herbert Walker Bush. And Paul with a ponytail down to his waist is great. You can tell him the most idiotic joke (I did) and he'll give it a big ol' belly laugh.

The afternoon light is waning and it's time to go. Mike and Paul tell me about a cheap motel in Mankato, which is about twenty miles east. Before I turn in for the night, I have a fine steak dinner at the Buffalo Roam Steak House and top it off with two pieces of the tastiest gooseberry pie.

A sincere word about Kansas. Whatever it lacks in spectacular, in-your-face, Yosemite/Yellowstone-type beauty is made up by the people in it. They're aware of their "Bleeding Kansas" history and how they not only survived it but prospered despite it. They have no urge or need for boasting, and are a perfect example of "Keep your word, keep your peace, and do what's right." It's an easy place to feel comfortable, to feel at home, to feel like you belong. Kansas is uniquely sublime and I couldn't be happier here. We Americans are fortunate to have it.

My original plan was to go south through Oklahoma and arrive in Dallas, Texas on Saturday but then I find out that I don't need to be there until Sunday. Ah! An extra day! I point The Beast eastward and off we go to Kansas City, a fabled and fundamental thread in the American tapestry. It's part of countless songs and poems and histories but what interests me most today is that it's Charlie Parker's hometown and home to the American Jazz Museum at 18th and Vine.

I clumsily navigate my way through downtown Kansas City, and when I get to 18th and Vine, it's just the neatest place. When I walk into the museum, I find a big, happy surprise waiting. The Negro Baseball Leagues Museum is right across the lobby! Are you kidding me? Jazz and baseball in one building! Could it be any more perfect? Neither museum is very large but they're both so, so well done. I walk over to the baseball side and I'm taken to another time. The photos alone, all those beautiful faces, tell the story, the beautiful story of baseball and an indelible culture. Other stories are told as well, the ugly stories of racism and bigotry, but the beauty of baseball and those who played it and loved it carry the day.

I go over to the Jazz side. At first, I'm overcome with emotion and just stand there a while, as if I've wandered onto hallowed ground. I begin to amble around and look at the displays and see one of Ella's sequined dresses, one of Duke's suits, and an old musicians' union contract for a Bird and Diz concert in New York in 1948. There are stools you can sit on and listen with headphones to many of the greats: Satchmo and Sidney, the Count and the Duke, the Prez and the Hawk and the Brute, Ella and Sarah and Mel, Cannonball and Nat, Trane and Miles, Monk and Mingus and Oscar; and I have to mention Clifford, whose worst solo was outstanding.* During the long while I listen, the only time in the universe is in the music itself.

Then I find *the* track, the track that *makes* my visit: Bird and Diz ripping through *Shaw 'Nuff*. I close my eyes and there is nothing but those magnificent notes and the joy that accompanies them. I remain mesmerized long after it's over.

Together, those Jazz greats, along with hundreds of others delivered a world-wide sucker punch to musical complacency and never stopped swinging. But the most powerful, the most unavoidable, the most devastating right cross came from Bird himself. He was/is one of those rare musicians, rare artists, who actually change your life, change the way you think, change the way you look at yourself and your musicianship. He probably had more effect on Jazz than any other musician, which means more effect on American music in general. He definitely had an enormous effect on me. When I first heard him, I was in awe and fright, as all of us were.

If you pick up a book about Bird's life, you'll read about the alcohol abuse and all the gigs he missed because of it. You'll read about how he sold his saxes in order to buy heroin and would have to play a plastic sax on street corners in Los Angeles for pocket change. Busking it's called. You'll read about how he was committed to the Camarillo State Mental Hospital for six months. You'll read about his death at the age of thirty-four, but the coroner, not knowing who he was, estimated his age to be between sixty and sixty-five.

But you'll also read about how he practiced, then practiced, then practiced some more. How he never held a Jazz-only attitude, sometimes playing with Country-Western bands; how he listened to and studied the music of Igor Stravinsky, his favorite Classical composer. How he ceaselessly explored the upper realms of melody and harmony and rhythm. How he never, ever stopped experimenting or looking for perfection. How he constantly lived and breathed all he had discovered and dreamed about, sometimes, I believe, morphing into the very music itself. And when he played, oh my, when he played it all came out, every ounce of sweat and humanity and wisdom. And it was glorious.

Despite the alcohol and drugs, the racism and bigotry, the cold nights and lonely days, and the hunger and pain, he never stopped playing. And he played only one note at a time. Think about that a moment. Here was a man with no marketing and no advertising behind him, no demographic studies, no surveys and no benefactors to forward his career and make him famous and rich; a man who played only *one note at a time*, most of them in obscurity, yet he changed the course of music forever.

When you consider all of it, there are many lessons we can learn from Bird. Lessons about technical mastery, musical expression, aesthetic depth; lessons about perseverance and artistic integrity and holding fast to a forward-leaning philosophy. Perhaps, however, the deepest, longest lasting and most important lesson is a simple one: Wherever your heart resides, go there.

*

BIRD ... CHARLES PARKER, JR. (1920-1955); ALTO SAX

DIZ ... JOHN BIRKS GILLESPIE (1917-1993); TRUMPET

SATCHMO ... LOUIS ARMSTRONG (1901-1971); TRUMPET

SIDNEY ... SIDNEY BECHET (1897-1959); CLARINET, SAX

THE COUNT ... WILLIAM BASIE (1904-1984); PIANO

THE DUKE ... EDWARD KENNEDY ELLINGTON (1899-1974); PIANO

THE PREZ ... LESTER WILLIS YOUNG (1909-1959); TENOR SAX

THE HAWK ... COLEMAN RANDOLPH HAWKINS (1904-1969); TENOR SAX

THE BRUTE ... BENJAMIN FRANCIS WEBSTER (1909-1973); TENOR SAX

ELLA ... ELLA JANE FITZGERALD (1917-1996); SINGER

SARAH ... SARAH LOIS VAUGHN (1924-1990); SINGER

MEL ... MELVIN HOWARD TORMÉ (1925-1999); SINGER

CANNONBALL ... JULIAN EDWIN ADDERLY (1928-1975); ALTO SAX

NAT ... NATHANIEL ADDERLY (1931-2000); TRUMPET

TRANE ... JOHN WILLIAM COLTRANE (1926-1967); TENOR AND SOPRANO SAX

MILES ... MILES DEWEY DAVIS, III (1926-1991); TRUMPET

MONK ... THELONIUS SPHERE MONK (1917-1982); PIANO

MINGUS ... CHARLES MINGUS, JR. (1922-1979); BASS

OSCAR ... OSCAR EMMANUEL PETERSON (1925-2007); PIANO

CLIFFORD ... CLIFFORD BROWN (1930-1956); TRUMPET

14

LOVE AFFAIRS

She walks in beauty like the night
Of cloudless climes and starry skies,
And all that's best of dark and bright
Meet in her aspect and her eyes;
Thus mellowed to the tender light
Which heaven to gaudy day denies.

—Byron

On this particular trip, I enter Arizona from the northeast on US Highway 160 and pass by the small towns of Teec Nos Pas, Red Mesa, Dennehotso, Kayenta and Tonalea. I always enjoy the names of towns and cities and wonder about the histories behind them. I also create loopy word games, like Dennehotso becomes "Denny Hot? So...?" And Kayenta spelled backwards is Atneyak, which sounds like a name for a town above the Arctic Circle in Northern Canada.

The 160 is fairly straight and there aren't any memorable sights, but because I'm in the mood to get in some miles it suits me just fine. During most of the ride there's a cold, hard rain but I'm making good time anyway. When I'm ready to bed down for the night, I come to an area that comprises four small towns. They each have an interesting name and I wonder how they came together in their odd, eclectic group: Rare Metals, Moenave, Moenkopi, and Tuba City.

I pull into a motel in Tuba City and there are about twenty motorcycles, most of them Harleys, parked in the dirt and gravel parking lot. There's also a trailer hitched to a pickup. I talk with the fellow who owns the pickup and it turns out he's the guide for those twenty bikers, who are from Poland and touring the American Southwest on rented bikes. What a terrific thing to do! So I walk on over. Only a few know a handful of English words and I know no Polish, but with riding long distances in common, we manage to have a pleasant back-and-forth.

In the morning, I'm switched around direction-wise so I ask the ill-tempered girl at the front desk for directions to Sedona, and she tells me to go back out to Highway 160 and turn left. While packing up, I begin to think I ought to turn right but I'm not one of those people who can always point true north (I easily get lost, in other words) so I go back and ask if she's sure it's a left turn to Sedona. She's even more ill-tempered now and growls, "Yes!", then turns around and walks away.

I leave my room key on the desk, get on my bike, go out to the 160 and turn left. I ride for about twenty miles in Navajo country but it still seems like I should have turned right, so I stop at a market/gas station and ask an older fellow, who's sitting out front and wearing a hat with a feather in it, how to get to Sedona. He doesn't know. He asks me to repeat Sedona a few times and it's clear he has no idea where it is. Or even what it is. Actually, I don't think he knows where *he* is.

Then he asks me for $1.67. I wonder at the odd amount but don't ask. So I reach into my pocket and pull out all my cash. I have two twenties, a five, two ones and forty-seven cents in change. He grabs my hand and carefully fingers through it all. I'm willing to give him two bucks, even five, but he gets a disgusted look on his face and says, "There's just forty-seven cents." I offer him the two one-dollar bills and he impatiently repeats that he needs $1.67. Then he angrily waves me off and walks away.

It reminds me of an old joke. Joe and Mo want to escape from an insane asylum. They're on the fifth floor and figure if they can get enough bed sheets and tie them together end to end, they can climb down to freedom. So they pilfer a bunch of bed sheets and tie them together. They wait until after midnight so they won't be seen, then tie one end to the bedpost and throw the other end out of the window. Before escaping, they need to make sure the rope of bed sheets is long enough, so they flip a coin to see who'll be the one to find out. Mo loses. He's scared but bravely begins his descent and quickly gets swallowed up in the darkness. About an hour later he climbs back through the window totally exhausted. Joe asks him what happened. Mo finally catches his breath and says, "It ain't gonna work." "Why not?" Joe asks. "It's too long."

I walk into the market and one of the cashiers, a cheerful Navajo teenager, gives me clear directions and, sure enough, the girl at the motel had steered me wrong. So I backtrack to Tuba City. Only now do I realize it's the same stretch of road I traveled yesterday but didn't recognize it because it had been raining so hard. It's a two-lane highway with a fair amount of traffic so I settle in behind a car with two women in it. About seven or eight miles later a large, colorful cloth blows out of the passenger side window. I pull over and retrieve it while the car makes a U-turn and comes back. I run across the highway and the driver, a middle-aged Navajo woman, steps onto the narrow shoulder. Her skin is luminescent, her hair black and straight, her eyes round and soft. I'm taken. We stand close and still and can scarcely breathe. She smiles and the air sparkles.

She walks in beauty like the night
Of cloudless climes and starry skies ... .

Byron's lines silently swirl around her and like the transformations of a kaleidoscope, they soften the angles and warm the colors of the sunlight. I shed all things earthly and join her elevated world with sublime ambitions. With child-like fantasy, I protect her from wild winds, keep her unmarred as we touch the savage and unbroken, infuse her lofty passions with fiery pleasures. In her eyes, those deep and soft eyes, I see that she, too, yearns for the fiery pleasures of the wild and unbroken. Gradually, calm returns and again the lines from Byron swirl around her. *She walks in beauty like the night....*

Reluctantly, I gather my composure and gently hand her the cloth. She quietly says, "Thank you" and I manage to quietly say, "Of course." We hold the moment, two hands on one cloth. Finally, she shyly apologizes and says she must get her mother to a doctor's appointment. Our eyes part but the longing remains.

The Beautiful Navajo Woman makes another U-turn and I follow her, often seeing her pretty face as she smiles at me in the rear view mirror. When she turns right at Tuba City, I slow down and follow the car with my eyes as long as possible. It is our first and last goodbye. As I continue riding, I think about the Beautiful Navajo Woman and wonder over and over, what would have happened if...?

Though love affairs like this are brief, they are nonetheless true love affairs because they encompass all the dreams and out-of-breath fantasies of the longer kind. Though the moments and words are few, the unspoken thoughts and feelings are lasting and fulfilling. They happen at unpredictable times, like when you see someone in a car next to you on a freeway, or when you almost bump into someone walking out of a grocery store, or when you're standing behind someone in line at a coffee shop. There's a connection, an intimacy, an understanding; somehow personal histories are known and predilections understood. True, they end, but so do most love affairs no matter how long they last. (Blessed are those who find one that lasts forever, something I once did.) Besides, of what importance is time in matters of love? Love is timeless. Days, weeks, months and years mean nothing. Is the beauty of a sunset any less because it ends?

I make a left onto US Highway 89, which, scenery-wise, is much like the 160. I don't see much of Flagstaff when I get there because I directly get onto Interstate 40 then quickly onto Interstate 17 then about three miles later I get onto Highway 89A, which leads to Sedona, all the while thinking about the Beautiful Navajo Woman.

Soon, the 89A becomes more and more mountainous and the views become more and more picturesque. It's a fabulous road and I push my limits on every corner. However, just north of Sedona, I'm presented with a conflict that's common in such areas. Do I slow down and take in the view, or do I continue to slam-ride this great road like that's the only thing it was meant for? This time, I slow down.

Sedona is one of "those" places. You've heard about "those" places for years and years. They're the ones that friends tell you about over and over and when you finally go, you find out it's more beautiful, more remarkably beautiful, more unbelievably beautiful than everyone said it was. For a mountain area, Sedona is fairly well-populated (over ten thousand), but there must be some strict zoning regulations because everything is either placed so it's unnoticeable, or designed so it fits right in with the natural environment. Really, if you haven't been to

Sedona, drop everything and go. Right now. Just go. If you *have* been to Sedona, you know what I'm talking about and you're already planning your next trip, I know it.

I pull into a long, narrow turnout covered with gravel. At the near end is a wooden building shared by a souvenir store and a fast food joint where burgers and deep-fried chicken are the specialties. All along the back of the turnout are tables covered with more souvenirs, faux Indian jewelry and various mountain-style knick-knacks, and in the middle of it all is a guy selling maps. I park at the far end of the turnout next to a light blue bus, which has something about youth camps painted on the side.

I check out all the merchandise as I slowly amble toward the fast food joint, where I'm going to buy a well-deserved vanilla ice cream cone. When I get to the door, fifteen children and a counselor from the blue bus are behind me. The counselor is wearing a backpack and carrying a light blue suitcase. Over the years, I've learned that innocently stating the obvious almost always gets a chuckle, assuming that the other person has, at the least, a small sense of humor. So I observe, "Say! You're carrying a light blue suitcase!" He doesn't react in the slightest, not even a frown or a scowl, and continues to stare straight ahead as if he's trying hard to pretend I don't exist. I hold the door open for him and the campers, figuring that, you know, it's the polite thing to do.

I get inside and the counselor is vigorously herding the kids into two lines, which means I have to wait for the counselor and fifteen kids to make up their minds and order and pay before I can get my vanilla ice cream cone. I do the math: sixteen people at, say, three minutes per order divided by two cashiers equals twenty-four minutes of waiting. At least. If I go first, it's only a three-minute wait and there'd still be another cashier available. All I want is an ice cream cone. The counselor doesn't know that, of course, but even if I order a full meal, how long does it take one guy to order and pay? It would be courteous, I think, if the counselor would tell me to go ahead of them, and it would set a good example for the kids. I stand around for a minute or so hoping he'll change his mind but he's still pretending I don't exist, so I go back outside and talk with the guy selling maps.

The map seller is bright, friendly and talkative. He tells me he used to ride but quit after going down and breaking a leg, an arm and a few ribs, which was only days after his girlfriend left him. I commiserate. We've all been there; not necessarily the broken bones part, but the girlfriend part. He also tells me about some great Sedona roads to ride, marks them on a map and gives it to me. A half an hour later, the counselor and the kids have all ordered and paid for their food, and I finally get my vanilla ice cream cone.

I'm ready to take off as the counselor and his kids are coming back to the bus. He doesn't want to cross my path – it's dangerous, you never know what we fiendish bikers will do – so he stops and waits for me to leave. In the spirit of quid pro quo, I'm so, so carefully slow as I back out.

The traffic is snarled well before downtown Sedona. It's only four or five blocks long but it takes a half an hour to get to the other side of town because the cars are so closely bunched together and there's no room to split lanes. Besides, lane-splitting is illegal in Arizona. (As if that would stop me.)

The slow traffic isn't too bothersome, however, because I love Sedona, as probably everyone who visits does. The residents, too. How could you not? Downtown is a relaxing, artistic place with unique eateries and gift shops and a lot of places that sell some incredible artwork and amazing sculptures by local artists. However, today my interest is the area outside of town. I want to find a great place to photograph the sunset, which I'm certain will be legendary. I'd tucked away the free map in my bag but don't stop to get it out because I prefer exploring without a definite route in mind. I ride around, see a few neighborhoods and finally, southwest of town, find Red Rock Loop Road, which leads to a valley of sorts, and it's ideal. There are a couple of hours before sunset so I ride back to find something to eat.

I've a hankering for another vanilla ice cream cone and walk into an AM/PM mini-mart. (Yes, I have a deep fondness, a love if you will, for vanilla ice cream cones.) Their ice cream machine is broken but the lady behind the counter is an easy conversation so I get her to tell me about Sedona. The most interesting thing is that because of the local no-garish-ness regulations, little Sedona (I love this) forced goliath McDonald's to back down and put green arches on their building instead of those tacky yellow ones. She claims that it's the only McDonald's in the world with green arches. This is something I have to see, plus I know McDonald's sells ice cream cones, and she gives me directions. It's on the same street only a couple or three blocks away. Funny thing though, I ride past it three times before I see it. I guess those tacky yellow arches do have a use.

I go back to Red Rock Loop Road and wait for the sure-to-be spectacular sunset. There are a number of homes about a mile south of me and when the local residents drive by, they all smile as if to say, "We know. You're standing there waiting for the sunset." The wait is worth it. I can't take photos fast enough. The sky to the east is molten with every imaginable shade of purple constantly weaving into and around one another, as if it's being watercolored by a giant, invisible hand. The sky to the west is mythically luminescent with blues and whites and yellows and oranges. For a magical five minutes, a horizontal strata in the low cliffs a couple of hundred yards away glows bright orange as if lit from inside.

I ride out of my little valley-of-the-sunset and stop when I reach the 89A where, for no particular reason, I decide to spend the night in Prescott. I look back toward Sedona, smile and promise to someday return. The post-sunset air is comfortable. Standing in it, I reflect on the serendipity of meeting the Beautiful Navajo Woman, and how it all began with getting wrong directions. I take a fancy to the notion that the growling girl at the motel intentionally did me a favor, that she somehow knew that a colorful cloth would fly out of a window and I would retrieve it. Wistful for the Beautiful Navajo Woman, I close my eyes. My thoughts go to the unforgettable sunset and how I would like to have given it to her as a gift. Then I think that what it really was, was a gift *from* the Beautiful Navajo Woman. Or that, perhaps, she *is* the unforgettable sunset itself. I like that.

Sedona to Prescott via Interstate 17 is sixty-six miles but I decide to stay on Highway 89A, a route that's a little shorter, but that's not my reason. I take the 89A because it leads through the town of Jerome, which is supposed to have a spectacular view. (I know, I know, it's going to be nighttime and I won't be able see any of the view, but hey, I'm lightheaded in love so I ignore that commonsense rationale.) The 89A also leads through the mountains. Starting at under four thousand feet, it goes up to over seven thousand feet and back down. The road is in great shape but it's cold, dark (the sliver of a moon is almost always behind clouds), raining most of the time, and the wind is blowing from every which way.

A little anxiety sets in when I see a few signs that tell me to watch for small animals. Also, the cold, nighttime mountain air has gotten to me and I'm constantly fighting the urge to shiver uncontrollably. Wouldn't it be nice, I think, if the Beautiful Navajo Woman was sitting on the back of my bike, arms wrapped around me and keeping me warm and calm by whispering beautiful Navajo poetry in my ear?

Every ten minutes or so there's a car coming the other way filled with young people laughing and singing. Other than that, I'm alone. Toward the top, I start seeing mountain houses with steeply angled roofs. (I don't know but I'm thinking this is Cottonwood.) A little later I turn a corner and there's Jerome, all lit up, music coming out of the restaurants, and people sauntering about and having a good time. It takes a short while to adjust because it's *so* different from what I've just been through, and so different from what I'd expected, which was a quiet, sleepy mountain village. I'm stirred by the profuse festivities.

I'm also cold, tired and hungry and the sensible thing to do is find a hot meal and a warm, comfortable bed. But I decide to keep riding, for some non-sensible reason bound to my earlier decision of making it to Prescott. (It's funny how we sometimes suffer hazards and pain just because of a knuckleheaded obedience to a past decision, even a decision based on nothing but whim.) The road is narrow and lined with parked cars and it doesn't feel like I'm on a highway anymore so I ask for directions from four jovial ladies who are walking along the sidewalk. They tell me not to worry and just keep going.

I zigzag my way out of Jerome and begin the descent, which is so zigzagging that it makes a Mobius strip look like a laser beam. Now I'm really cold and hungry and tired when I could be, should be, enjoying a hot dinner in a warm mountain restaurant. Instead, I pull over and eat the last of my beef jerky. Knuckleheaded obedience.

The jerky keeps me sated for only a few minutes before the cold, fatigue and hunger begin to bury into my very core. After what seems like three hundred hours, I'm in a flat area. The 89A has become a broad parkway but I immediately run into some road construction and for a couple of miles I'm riding on nothing but the underbed of gravel. It's tough. My whole body is stiff and aching, I'm wobbling all over the place, and I'm on the verge of hallucinating.

What seems like decades later, I make a left, then another left, and roll into Prescott around 10 P.M. beat up, starved and lead-dog tired. I see a Motel 6 and all I can think is "Ah, luxury!" You're right, there's no connection between luxury and a Motel 6, but it's the only thought I can muster up so I go with it. The vacancy sign is not working, so I go inside and ask the sweet desk lady, a mother of four, if there are any vacancies.

Sweet Desk Lady, Mother of Four: I have only one room left but there's no bed in it.

Me: *(Mind not working, staring, mouth half open)*

Sweet Desk Lady, Mother of Four: I'll give you a $20 discount.

Me: *(Mind still not working, still staring, mouth still half open)*

Sweet Desk Lady, Mother of Four: I'll give you all the blankets and pillows you want.

Me: *(Mind hears the word "pillows")* Oh, I am *so* down for that!

I get to my bed-less room and order pizza. As soon as I hang up, I remember that I have been forever plagued with a pizza oddity. *Every* time I order pizza, it *never* tastes as good as when someone else orders it. In my more incoherent moments, such as the one I'm in now, I imagine some sort of cosmic decree, imperiously handed down trillions of years ago by a deranged demigod I had angered: HENCEFORTH, WHENEVER THOU SHALT ORDER PIZZA, IT SHALL BE BAD PIZZA! I resign myself to eating bad pizza for dinner and, sure enough, that's what I get. While chewing the leathery crust, I close my eyes to visions of the Beautiful Navajo Woman. If she were here, right now, she would have ordered the pizza and it would be heavenly. I go to sleep in my sleeping bag amid a confusion of pillows.

I wake up surprisingly refreshed, skip breakfast and ride Highway 89 South out of Prescott and into the Prescott National Forest. Now *this* is fun! For one thing, it's daytime and I can actually see, and what I see is spectacular. There are so many twisties in the first sixteen miles that you could scrape your pegs down to nubs inside of a week. It straightens out in Peeples Valley then hits some more mountains. After Yarnell, the road divides, meaning it splits in two, meaning I'm on constantly winding asphalt maybe fifteen feet wide and what seems like a thousand feet above the valley floor, which makes me feel like I'm flying. But I'm not flying, I'm riding a motorcycle. So I try to concentrate on my riding, meaning look where I'm going, but what I really want to do is look at the view and feel like I'm flying, which is what I do several times, which isn't a good thing because I momentarily go out of control and actually get scared, something that hasn't happened since I don't know when. But boy, what a thrill!

At the town of Congress I stay on the 89, which is now mostly straight, then merge with the mostly straight US Highway 93. A short while later I'm in Wickenburg eating another vanilla ice cream cone and drinking two wake-you-up limeades. From there I head west on the also mostly straight US Highway 60.

The temperature is perfect for riding and there's very little traffic. Mountains are always in the distance, the Arizona flatlands rest heavily and the cloud-laden sky is made tough by the steel-like quality in all the colors. It's along this stretch that my emotions expand. I stop alongside the road, find a rock to sit on and think about love affairs and the Beautiful Navajo Woman. Again I ask myself, "What would have happened if...?"

15

CRAZY HORSE

Nations, like individuals, are punished for their transgressions.

—Ulysses S Grant

It will have blood, they say: blood will have blood.

—Shakespeare

I first learned of Crazy Horse in a short story I read in summer school before fifth grade. I don't recall anything about the story itself but I do have vivid memories of how I felt afterward, how I changed. Going out into those fields around our neighborhood became a different experience; what had been nothing more than meandering walks had become a high adventure. My bow and arrow became sacred. I took them out of my overcrowded closet and put them in a special place on top of my chest of drawers. I even did extra chores so I could buy a new, stronger bow and more arrows. But though I practiced and practiced and tried and tried, I could never shoot flying grasshoppers or even a slow moving opossum.

PART I

There is a feeling of adventure when you're out riding. Not to the degree of, say, gold miners venturing into 19th Century Yukon Territory, or of early settlers homesteading on the edge on Comanche country, or of Crazy Horse riding across the plains with a passel of stolen horses, but it's there, that sense of adventure *is* there. True, our hazards are mild compared to theirs but they *are* hazards nonetheless. (They'd probably laugh at our dismay over a broken bungee strap.)

I often mention Crazy Horse, one of the stellar characters in North American history, because he embodies so much I admire, the greatest being constancy. It's interesting that so much of what Crazy Horse epitomizes is so much of what we Americans feel epitomizes America: charity, courage, intelligence, competence, fidelity, perseverance, incorruptibility and a tenacious insistence on freedom. It's ironic because it was America, more accurately the government of America, who did so much to butcher the freedom of the Plains Indians, the freedom Crazy Horse loved and lived.

By the end of the 1860s the overwhelming numbers of Whites, the military campaigns of the US Army, and the broken promises and spirit-crippling reservation life created by the US government had wiped out the traditional ways of life for most of the Plains Indians. A number of things led to this state of affairs. White writers, masquerading as journalists, misrepresented the Plains Indians as nothing but violent, unpredictable maniacs, which led to an unrealistic fear and hatred of them. The Civil War had just ended with over six hundred thousand deaths in only four years. That's an average of over 410 deaths a day (*over 410 deaths a day!*) so when news came of a battle where there were thirty or so combined deaths, occasionally over a hundred, it didn't have the impact on the post-Civil War population that it normally would have had. Then there was the matter of gold. The Whites wanted it and the Indians were simply "in the way." There were other things, too, but the point is that it had all the ingredients of an inexorable tragedy.

The tragedy for the Plains Indians is easy to see and there are countless books and articles written about it. But it is also a tragedy for all of America, even now, over a century later, because those transgressions against so much of what we hold dear (an insistence on freedom and the other virtues I mentioned above) necessarily undermine those things for all of us, and this is something we as a country continue to wrangle with.

(None of this is intended to claim that the Plains Indians sat around being victims. They didn't. They fought and fought well, their warrior elite being among the best this planet has ever seen. I don't know when Sun Tzu's *Art of War* was available in North America but the Plains Indian warriors seem to have had a thorough working knowledge of everything in it. Too, we mustn't forget that there are many cases of the Plains Indians committing egregiously, unprovoked violent acts against the Whites.)

It would be absurd to claim that I'm an adventurer on the level with Crazy Horse, but when I'm out riding I do feel a kinship with him. True, I'm rumbling along a paved highway at 60-90 mph instead of on the back of a horse making maybe fifty miles a day, but I *am* chasing the same clouds, looking at the same mountains and catching the same wind; and when I lie down to sleep on the ground, the same moon and stars give me comfort. Some may consider the analogy farfetched and in a way there's truth in that view. There are many differences between Crazy Horse's yearly treks in the 19th Century and my paved wanderings in the 21st, but there are similarities as well and it's on those that I focus. Besides, when it comes to the high sensations of adventure and freedom, logic assumes its proper lower order and, as such, is irrelevant.

I believe it was the 18th Century Swiss philosopher Rousseau who first pointed out that the Plains Indians had a highly workable form of non-government. If someone didn't want to engage in a raid, he could simply opt out. If the chiefs said it was time to move to better hunting grounds for the winter but someone wanted to wait a few weeks, he could stay where he was without penalty. Others might think him daft and try to persuade him, but no one had the authority to *force* him to travel. And therein is the crux. The idea of governmental enforcement was not part of the Plains Indians' way of life. The idea that anyone had authority over anyone else just never took hold.

On the other hand, one of the consistent aspects of White civilizations is government. There has always been a leader or group of leaders (presidents, legislatures, kings, dictators, parliaments, etc.) that have been vested with the authority to establish and enforce laws, coin money, make treaties, levy taxes, wage war, enforce conscription, and so forth. While reading Larry McMurtry's wonderful little book on Crazy Horse, I realized that one exception to this, possibly the only one, is my own heritage, the Vikings, and this is another point of concordance I have with Crazy Horse. (There are many similarities between Plains Indian culture and Viking culture.) But while that is a personal concordance, I believe it's one shared by anyone who loves freedom, which includes anyone who regularly rides a motorcycle.

Too, there is a broader concordance between motorcyclists and the 19th Century Plains Indians. If you're a rider or passenger, you can dress up or dress down; you can cover yourself with tattoos or have none at all; you can ride a pristine, beautifully painted bike or one that never gets washed. You can ride alone or with a group, but even if you're with a group, you can pull over whenever and wherever you want and decide to go back home. There's no right or wrong way to be or look like or talk like or think like a biker. When you're around other bikers, everyone "is what they is" and respected for it. It's remarkable that with the vast diversity of personalities, religions, races, and political affiliations among bikers, there are relatively so few fights and arguments.

When you're riding, there is this undeniable feeling of self-reliance and self-authority over your own actions, your own life. That pavement rolling by a foot or so under your boots represents death or, at the least, serious injury, so it could be no other way. True, there are dangers inherent in driving a car but the penalties for making a wrong decision are far less. If you get into a fender bender in a car, you climb your way out of the airbag and call a tow truck; on a bike, someone else calls an ambulance and you might spend the rest of your life in a wheelchair. This is the reason bikers have, or quickly develop, a sense of self-reliance and self-authority.

Self-reliance and self-authority are vital foundations of true freedom. To get there, the *only* two factors to resolve are *who* has authority over you, and *on whom* do you rely, you yourself or someone else. When you're on a motorcycle, there's really no choice. You're either self-reliant, assume authority over yourself and keep riding, or eventually land in the hospital at the mercy of doctors and insurance companies.

This is not to say that we never accept or offer help. We do and we do it a lot. But when we accept or offer help, it's never at the expense of our own or someone else's self-reliance or self-authority. The reason it's like that is because the help we give and receive is done with no enforcement. We help because we *want to,* not because we have to. And therein is the essence.

When help is freely proffered, it works and works wonderfully, for both the giver and receiver. It's fun and satisfying. When help is enforced, however, it *may* work but only temporarily. After that will come an inevitable decline of morale and an inevitable increase of resentment, fraudulence and bigotry. This is one of the primary reasons why the Plains Indians and the Viking culture remained, for the most part, pure and thriving. Same thing with the motorcycle community.

In his marvelous book *Twelve Against the Gods*, William Bolitho wrote, "We are born free as eagles, yet we are cursed to stay and dig." Stay and dig, indeed. Holding down a job or two or three, going to meetings, paying taxes, paying bills, paying back loans. Add to it all those things others persuade and require us to do, plus the *unthinking* enforcement of ever-growing and *unnecessary* laws and regulations, and we have a society in which there is a constant undermining of self-reliance and self-authority. Perforce, our freedoms constantly erode. So what do you do? The government is not going away and neither are your creditors. How to you escape this endless digging? Well, one perfect antidote is to be a motorcyclist, a rider, a biker. (Fortunately, it's still legal.) It's a simple solution that sounds simplistic, and perhaps it is, but it *does work.* The only proviso is keeping at it.

But what of this assumption of self-authority and the common laws we "must" obey? Bikers and other freedom-loving people recognize that laws exist and that many of them are good ideas. Stop at the stop sign, don't cross the double yellow line, don't park in the handicapped zone. But while we admit the existence of those laws and the usefulness of many of them, the inherent hazards of riding a motorcycle, and by extension the inherent hazards of freedom, real freedom, are such that many of those laws simply are not necessary for us.

That's not to say that we defy the law. Well sometimes yes, but what I mean to say is that we don't violate the reasons, the underlying concepts, for the laws. For instance, it's a law to use a turn signal or hand signal when turning or changing lanes. It's a good idea but if no one else is around, what's the use? I often change lanes without using a turn signal but every time I do, I've determined from direct observation that it's not needed. But what if someone decides that they'll always use a turn signal when changing lanes, whether anyone else is around or not? As long as he's making that decision *himself* and *not only* because it's a law, then it's fine. But if he's doing it *only* because it's a law, then he's undermined his own self-authority and eventually will suffer because of it.

It's not a matter of operating outside the law, it's a matter of being so free and responsible that you don't need the law.

As a side note, regarding the mistaken indispensability of laws, I can't count the number of times I've been to a biker joint where the parking lot, if you could call it that, is nothing but dirt and rock; no traffic signs, no marked parking spaces or pathways, no one directing traffic, pedestrians crisscrossing constantly. These are lawless areas but there is rarely, very rarely, a mishap.

Whenever I hear someone say that motorcycling is dangerous, a sentiment that's easy to understand, I always think of a paraphrase of something Helen Keller wrote: Safety is mostly a superstition. (Ms. Keller used the word security.) There are two commonsense ways to look at motorcycling. One is that riding is not a safe activity, never was, never will be. There are many things you can do to make it less dangerous, of course, and you should do all of them, but the rudimentary activity of it is simply not safe. The other is this: Riding is not, of itself, inherently dangerous. It is, however, unforgiving of inattention, ignorance, incompetence, and stupidity.

If you think it through, these are two ways to state the same concept, the second one being far more clever, and not surprisingly they apply to life in general. If you agree with Ms. Keller, and I do, living itself is not safe. Or you could say it the other way, that living is unforgiving of inattention, ignorance, incompetence, and stupidity. But getting back to motorcycling, all this talk of safety begs the question: Why do it? Well, for one thing, riding is so much damned fun. Then there are all those biker sayings, most of which are absolutely true. Four wheels move the body, two wheels move the soul. It takes more love to share a saddle that it does to share a bed. You'll never see a motorcycle parked outside a therapist's office. Put your knees in the breeze and your troubles disappear in your rearview mirror. Whatever it is, it's better in the wind. Oh, they go on and on.

My favorite biography on Crazy Horse is the one by Joseph M. Marshall III, himself a Lakota Sioux. While reading it, Crazy Horse became more real to me than ever before. He relates the tales about Crazy Horse he had heard as a boy from his elders, who had heard these tales from their elders who had actually seen and known Crazy Horse. It's a written record of an oral history. In cultures that have no oral tradition, such as present day America, word-of-mouth accounts are unreliable. (Let's face it, most written accounts in present day America are unreliable.) But in cultures that have a long oral tradition, such as Crazy Horse's Sioux, oral histories *are* reliable. As such, Marshall's biography is as close as I've ever come, as close as most all of us will ever come, to knowing Crazy Horse, the man himself.

Marshall writes about the battles, the killings, the hunts, even the uncertainties and missteps. Mostly what appealed to me was Crazy Horse's fidelity to his people and the Lakota way, which got me thinking of constancy, that invaluable but rarely mentioned virtue. It's a difficult one to attain, perhaps impossible, and I suspect that that's the reason it's rarely mentioned, but it's a good one to keep in mind, a goal to strive toward. Another aspect that Marshall elucidates is how Crazy Horse struggled with the divided responsibilities of providing for his family and hundreds of others, leading his warriors, and preserving the Lakota way, all while enjoying his own personal freedoms.

These responsibilities are paralleled in the biker community. First, I cannot think of a group that contributes to charity more consistently than bikers. In fact, I've never been to, or even heard of, a public biker rally that didn't have at least one fundraiser for a charity. Second, bikers who teach their kids to ride are *very* thorough and do not let them out on public roads until they're well skilled. Third, there are many, many organizations and individuals who defend the rights of bikers and educate the non-riding public.

Further, there is an agreed-upon rule that we never leave a stranded biker behind. I once saw an accident on a canyon near my home. I was coming up to a deceptive corner that is far harder to negotiate than what it seems, so I slowed down. A guy on a sports bike passed me and then another guy *passed him.* The second rider must have been going over 60 mph heading into a ninety degree turn that's wrongly banked. He didn't make it. He and his Ducati tumbled for thirty or forty yards and stopped when they hit a fence. He was passed out for a minute or so, but there were no broken bones and he was okay. The interesting thing is that *every* biker who came along stopped and asked if there was anything they could do to help. Within a half an hour there were about thirty of us standing around talking about bikes and riding. In that same time, about a dozen cars came by but none pulled over.

PART II

Wind. It's the first thing I notice about Wyoming. Incessant winds. I ask several residents if the wind ever stops and without hesitation they all give me a resigned "no." In all the other places I've ridden, hard and multi-directional winds like this feel like intrusions, like insults; in Wyoming they feel like part of the land, as if it's the one place they belong.

Despite the winds, I like Wyoming. A lot. You can buy fireworks year round, the license plates have a silhouette of a cowboy on a bucking bronco, the cloudscape is intricate and ever-changing, and the sky is powder blue to cobalt with every hue in between. It's a state with a lot of big animals: horses, camels, cows, (camels?) buffalo, antelope, (there are camels?) elk, deer, (yes, camels!) bears and a gazillion grasshoppers. (You might not consider grasshoppers to be large animals but, trust me, if you ever go to Wyoming you will.) It's a state with cattle guards at the freeway entrances. It's a state with town names like Bar Nunn, Greybull, Hoback and Medicine Bow. It's a state where a town (Hiland) with a population of under a hundred gets a spot on the map. Yeah, I like Wyoming. A lot. Despite the winds.

I'm rolling along on Interstate 25 North. Around Glendo, it begins heading west and at Casper it goes north again. But right there in Casper, on the spur of the moment, I decide to go northwest on US Highway 20, which is also US Highway 26. The road is in decent shape, there isn't much traffic, and the Western Wheatgrass waving in the wind massages my route. There's a grand, pioneering freedom here that fills your lungs every time you breathe. And the incessant winds? Well, a few times, they come from the left so strongly that they push my left nostril shut. It's the first time that's ever happened to me and I have to say it's an odd sensation. On the whole, though, I've gotten used to them so it now feels like I'm getting a full body massage. (At least, that's what I'm trying to convince myself of.)

Right before sundown, I hit the southern end of Boysen State Park, stay on the 20, which is also Highway 789 now, and start going north. (At this point, the 26 continues east.) It's a little mountainous and I catch some nice views of the Boysen Reservoir, then head through some boulder-lined canyons. There aren't any twisties but it's a fun ride, and I begin to think that this route was specifically designed for a relaxed cruise. Later, as the dusk is waning, I come upon another Wyoming characteristic: a constant enfilade of insects. I must have killed a million of them inside of twenty minutes. If there was ever a time and place to keep your mouth shut....

To my left is the constantly winding Wind River. I try to make a pun with "wind" as in what you do with a watch, and "wind" as in what the air is always doing in Wyoming, but nothing witty is forthcoming. I assuage the dismay over my witty-ness failure with the reasoning that I'm on the watch for deer crossing because that's what the signs say to do.

So I'm watching for deer, watching for deer, watching for deer when, aha!, there he is, over on the left, looking at me like, "Dude, let's play a game of chicken!" I'm seriously not interested so I slow down and he crosses about thirty yards away. No big deal, right? Then his buddy (sneaky little devil) jumps up out of the tall grass not twenty feet away and scares the bejesus out of me. I brake hard then swerve to the left missing his furry, pure-white butt by less than a foot. I think about spanking him but don't, figuring he learned his lesson. Later, I'm on the phone and mention the incident to my sister, who lives in the Texas hill country. She tells me, "Oh don't you know, Sweetie? There's *never* just one deer." Guess I'm the one who learned a lesson.

I spend the night in Thermopolis, which has these amazing hot springs, and in the morning continue on Highways 20 and 789. At Worland I take US Highway 16 through Tensleep, a friendly looking small town with one of the better names ever invented, and cut across the southern end of Bighorn National Monument, which is spectacular. At Buffalo, I get on Interstate 90 and that's when I first notice a change.

The change is a personal one, subtle and gradual. The rolling hills, the jagged mountains, the mesas in the distance, the cottonwoods lining the innumerable creeks and rivers are all fetching, but somehow I feel like I don't belong here. Other people look at me that way, too, and when I look at them they avoid my eyes. They don't want to talk to me and some act as if I'm not there at all. It's a feeling I seldom encounter and I don't know what to make of it or what to do about it. I ride and ride anyway, and take more photos, but the expected enjoyments elude me and I feel more and more like an unwelcome outsider.

I cross over the border into Montana, go to the site of the Battle of Little Bighorn and arrive there around 6 P.M. I walk around alone for a bit (still no one wants anything to do with me), take some photos, then head up the road that goes to the other end of the site. A hundred or so yards later the road is blocked but I go past it anyway to see if I can find a perfect spot for a sunset photo. A park ranger gives me a citation for entering a closed road, and another one fifteen minutes later for parking in a non-parking spot. I get a vicious bee sting on my right forearm.

I endure a restless sleep in a motel in Hardin and the following day I backtrack on Interstate 90, then ride about twenty miles east on US Highway 212, then south about twenty-five miles on County Road 314 to the Rosebud Battlefield site. The entrance has just one small sign and the road to the site itself is mostly dirt. It's only a mile and a half long but all the holes make it a rough go and it takes me ten minutes. When I arrive, there are only four other people there, but they soon leave and I have the entire place to myself. It's perfect. For a while I do nothing but sit and listen and look.

Sitting Bull had been a great warrior but by the 1870s, his warrior days were over and he had become a highly respected holy man. His extraordinary

VISION OF WHITE SOLDIERS FALLING OUT OF THE SKY INTO A LAKOTA VILLAGE WAS INTERPRETED TO MEAN THAT THE PLAINS INDIANS WOULD FINALLY STOP, ONCE AND FOR ALL, THE WESTWARD FLOW OF WHITE SETTLERS AND SOLDIERS, AND THAT THE SIOUX WAY OF LIFE WOULD BE PRESERVED FOREVER. THE NEWS OF THIS VISION QUICKLY SPREAD AND BY JUNE 1876, HE HAD ASSEMBLED AROUND TEN THOUSAND SIOUX, ARAPAHO AND NORTHERN CHEYENNE AT ASH CREEK, KNOWN TODAY AS RENO CREEK, JUST SOUTH OF THE LITTLE BIGHORN RIVER, WHICH THEY CALLED GREASY GRASS. IT WAS PERHAPS THE LARGEST EVER GATHERING OF PLAINS INDIANS. BETWEEN 1000 AND 2000 OF THESE WERE WARRIORS AND THEY WERE THE ONES WHO WOULD FIGHT THE US ARMIES.

THE US ARMY'S BASIC PLAN FOR THE BATTLE OF LITTLE BIGHORN WAS TO ATTACK SITTING BULL'S CAMP FROM THREE SIDES: GENERAL GIBBON FROM THE NORTH, GENERALS CUSTER AND TERRY FROM THE EAST, AND GENERAL CROOK, WHOM THE SIOUX CALLED THREE STARS, FROM THE SOUTH. BUT CUSTER WAS IMPETUOUS AND ATTACKED SITTING BULL'S CAMP BEFORE THE OTHER GENERALS ARRIVED, ONE OF SEVERAL ERRORS OF JUDGEMENT HISTORIANS HAVE BEEN POINTING OUT FOR YEARS. THE BATTLE OF LITTLE BIGHORN WAS FOUGHT ON JUNE 25TH AND 26TH, 1876, BUT THE FIRST DECISIVE BATTLE OCCURRED EIGHT DAYS EARLIER.

CRAZY HORSE'S SCOUTS HAD REPORTED GENERAL CROOK'S ADVANCE FROM THE SOUTH. THE CONSENSUS WAS THAT HE WAS THEIR BIGGEST THREAT FOR THREE REASONS. 1) HE WAS AN EXPERIENCED INDIAN FIGHTER; 2) DUE TO THE LOSSES HE SUFFERED DURING THE FETTERMAN INCIDENT, HE HAD A SCORE TO SETTLE WITH CRAZY HORSE AND THE SIOUX; AND 3) HIS WELL-SUPPLIED ARMY WAS THE ONE CLOSEST TO THEIR CAMP. CRAZY HORSE DECIDED TO TAKE THE BATTLE TO GENERAL CROOK INSTEAD OF WAITING FOR HIM TO ATTACK. THIS WOULD KEEP THE WOMEN, CHILDREN AND ELDERS SAFE AND HE WOULD BENEFIT FROM THE ELEMENT OF SURPRISE.

ON JUNE 17TH, AFTER A HARD, EARLY MORNING FIVE-MILE MARCH, CROOK AND HIS MEN RESTED ON THE SOUTH SIDE OF ROSEBUD CREEK NEAR WHAT WOULD BE THE SITE OF THE ROSEBUD BATTLE, WHICH THE INDIANS CALL THE BATTLE WHERE THE GIRL SAVED HER BROTHER. HE DID NOT POST SENTRIES BUT TO HIS GOOD FORTUNE, HIS CROW AND SHOSHONE SCOUTS RESTED UNEASILY ON THE NORTH SIDE.

ON THE NIGHT BEFORE, JUNE 16TH, CRAZY HORSE LED ABOUT 1500 WARRIORS FROM SITTING BULL'S CAMP. THEY BEGAN THE MARCH AFTER SUNDOWN AND RODE STRAIGHT THROUGH THE NIGHT, FORTY TO FORTY-FIVE MILES, AND CAME UPON THE ROSEBUD ENCAMPMENT A HALF AN HOUR AFTER CROOK. THEN, WITHOUT REST OR PAUSE (CAN YOU IMAGINE!), THEY ATTACKED. CROOK QUICKLY RALLIED HIS TROOPS AND FOR THE NEXT SIX HOURS THE HARD AND HEATED BATTLE OF ROSEBUD WAS FOUGHT.

I'm alone at the site of the Battle of Rosebud for a half an hour before my random thoughts fully subside. Time itself evanesces and it is then that I recreate the battle. Standing amid the Crow and Shoshone, I hear the distant thunder of hoofs then see two columns of Crazy Horse's men riding straight at me; Crazy Horse himself hanging off the side and shooting from under his horse's neck; his lifelong friends He Dog and Good Weasel doing the same.

The Crow and Shoshoni, though outnumbered, engage the Sioux and halt their advance. The soldiers quickly gather their horses and weapons then they, too, enter the fray. I see General Crook on a hill, issuing orders like a demigod and refusing to give in. And Captain Mills moving his men in attack and counterattack like a great conductor of great symphonies. It's pressed and loud. Of the battle, Mills wrote: The Indians proved then and there that they were the best cavalry on earth. Later, General Reno echoed the sentiment: The [Sioux and Cheyenne] Indians are the best light cavalry in the world. I have seen pretty nearly all of them and I do not except even the Cossacks.

After six hours of non-stop fighting, Crazy Horse, being low on ammunition and, more importantly, having accomplished his objective, which was to cripple Crook's forces, led his men back to Sitting Bull's camp at Ash Creek. (Later, they would all move to the Little Bighorn.) Crook claimed victory and because he still held Rosebud it was a technically accurate report. However, there's another side to it. (For one thing, Captain Mills wrote of the battle: We have been most humiliatingly defeated.) Because his resources had been depleted, Crook was forced to go back to his base camp at Goose Creek in Wyoming territory, where he had to wait almost two months for supplies. Perforce, he was unable to join Custer's army eight days later at the Battle of Little Bighorn. In that sense, the true victory belonged to Crazy Horse and his warriors.

As I leave, five deer accompany me to my right. Soon, they bound ahead, leap over a four-foot fence in unison, cross the road and descend into a ravine. When I reach the place of their crossing, I look to my left and they are already at the summit of a small hill a hundred yards away. One of them stops and looks back.

I go back to the site of the Battle of Little Bighorn. It's a fairly large place and the three-or-so mile road that was closed the day before is now open. I ride up. Not far from the end I come upon a passel of horses grazing by the side of the road. I stop and take a few photos then turn off the bike.

I watch them slowly coming my way, a few newborns among them. One of the horses, black with gray undertones, catches my attention and I call to him. He looks up. I tell him he reminds me of the type of battle horse the Sioux favored, mostly in the way he's alert to everything around him. He likes that and walks across the road and stands in front of me. He wants to know if my bike is alive and I tell him it is, but not in the way we usually think of life. He likes that, too, comes even closer and meticulously sniffs the entire front end. We have a long conversation, horse, iron horse and human, the subject matter private.

Finally, he comes right up to me, face-to-face, eye-to-eye, his lashes still chasing away flies. He takes in a long breath, shakes his head, snorts lightly, then trots off to join his friends. I fire up The Beast and ride to the end of the road.

On the way down, I read all the markers, which follow the actual flow of the battle. I watch General Reno attack the Sioux village to the west; I see Gall, that indomitable Hunkpapa Sioux warrior, and his men ride from the north and counterattack in full fury, Crazy Horse and his men not far behind. Reno, many of his men dead, retreats south and sets up skirmish lines where he is soon joined by Captain Benteen. Gall, seeing General Keogh attack from the east, redirects his warriors to counterattack. Crazy Horse rides farther north, where Custer had been shot from his horse just minutes before, and he and his warriors cross the Little Bighorn and attack Custer's men. I smell gunpowder and hear the death throes.

To the west, watching, is Sitting Bull. I *feel* his will. If his warriors fail, he and the other elders are the last defense for thousands of women and children. They are now too old for battle, but if it comes to them, they *will* fight and, if they must, die.

In the middle of it all, amid the thick smoke and cries of agony, time and again, I see Crazy Horse, untouchable and unflinching, slashing through the US Army like a thunder bolt from the Black Hills. I see a ridge with Keough's men on one side, Gall's on the other. The dead and the dying lay scattered across the battlefield under the haze and smell of burnt gunpowder. Custer's men, leaderless now, try to regroup on a small rise to the north, the warriors in furious pursuit. Suddenly, Crazy Horse, wearing a reddish-brown stone talisman behind his left ear and his face painted with a silver lightning bolt, rides directly through the middle of the soldiers, splitting them into two groups. The soldiers fire off all their rounds but even though he is only a few feet away, they all miss. Again he rides full tilt through the melee and again the bullets pass by him. The soldiers are awed and frustrated, the Indians inspired. One of the greatest warriors to have ever lived, he is at his finest: majestic and proud and flawless.

Crazy Horse and his brethren continue to relentlessly pursue the soldiers down into ravines and up blood-soaked hills, over the dead and through flurries of bullets. A few soldiers throw down their weapons and try to run away, but each is cut and killed like a small dirty animal, a fitting death for a coward. At last, three or so dozen soldiers, the last of Custer's men, are surrounded on a lone hill. The warriors, filled with bloodlust and triumph, do not pause. This is their greatest victory. The soldiers wait. They do not ask for mercy and will not surrender.

They die as they were meant to die,
As all men are meant to die,
Heated and bloodied with passions high.

I ride back to the visitor's center and the detachment I'd felt before is gone. Exactly when and why that happened I don't really know – well, I have my theories – but I do know that after my reenactments of the two battles, my emotions are calm, my thoughts tranquil. Now, as before, people smile, children shyly wave, and strangers start conversations. I am settled and will leave Montana with a light heart.

In life, we tend to pick sides in wars, arguments and even petty disagreements. I don't know if this is a natural thing to do, if it's part of our nature, but I do know it is prevalent. One value of studying history is that we don't *need* to pick sides. Nor should we. To truly understand history, we must be observers, not after-the-fact participants. That way, we *become* both sides and all of history belongs to us. To do otherwise is to dishonor those who actually fought, vanquished and victor alike.

But there are characters who capture our imaginations, with whom we associate in some way, and that's okay. For me, one of them is, obviously, Crazy Horse. He never sought the spotlight or encouraged others to sing his praises; he never bragged or even spoke about his accomplishments, and he gave the booty from his victories to the needy. I often think of him because, as I've said many times, he embodies so much I admire: charity, courage, intelligence, competence, fidelity, perseverance, incorruptibility and a tenacious insistence on freedom. And when I think of him I always think about his constancy. Throughout his life, all the way through his final moments, he remained true to himself, true to being free.

While writing about Crazy Horse, I often found myself wanting to inject phrases like "it seems to me" and "I think" and "my opinion is" and "I don't know, but…." One reason is because of the multitude of conflicting reports and opinions about the Plains Indians. Another reason is that there are many, many things I do not know about Crazy Horse. I've read a lot about him but can I say I truly know him? No. I've read a lot about Plains Indians' culture but do I truly know it? No. And I certainly have enough respect for both to not assume anything about either, something I hope I haven't done. Still another reason is that years ago I decided to cultivate the civilized ability to genuinely say, "I don't know," and since then I've become pretty good at it. All I've tried to convey here is how Crazy Horse has figured into my own life, my own thoughts, my own imaginings, my own dreams.

I've sometimes wondered why I am so drawn to Crazy Horse. Sure, there is the adventure, the excitement, the drama, and the intrigue, but there is something else, an intangible yet visceral yearning. There are others I'm drawn to in equivalent measure: Palestrina, Mozart, Ravel, Eleanor of Aquitaine, Isadora Duncan, Voltaire, Lola Montez, Oscar Wilde, and several others. But I can't fully explain why I'm drawn to them any more than I can fully explain why I'm drawn to Crazy Horse. In the end, I'm content with saying "I don't know." I'm content to say that because the reasons why are far less important than their influences and allowing myself to be altered in ways that make me a better man.

It is when I'm riding alone at night under the philosophy of the clouds, moon and stars that I think of Crazy Horse most often. Out there, somewhere out there, he yet rides and hunts and fights. I wish I could talk with him and hunt with him and fight alongside him. But then, perhaps I did. Perhaps I still do.

He outlives a million sunsets.

16

FREEDOMS

In much of my life's narrative, the margins have been far too wide.

I was born and raised in the San Joaquin Valley in Central California between the towns of Visalia and Exeter. Our house was five miles east of the Visalia city limits, a fact my dad would bring up every time someone told him that he had parked his car in front of our house pointed in the wrong direction. According to dad, this was illegal only *inside* the city limits so you couldn't get a ticket for it outside the city limits. I don't know if he ever did get a ticket but I like to think he didn't.

Our house was in what I've come to call a red, white and blue neighborhood: redneck, white trash and blue-collar. Though somewhat accurate, it's somewhat misleading as well. Our immediate neighborhood, three blocks of houses all built within a couple of years of each other, housed mostly blue-collar folks. Most of the hicks and white trash, along with the farmers, cowboys and rednecks, lived outside of those three blocks. However, all of us kids congregated at school and in pick-up baseball games where we each grappled in our own way with our little red, white and blue melting pot. And a thorough melting pot it was. Still today, there's a little of each of those in me.

It's a day in late spring and it is a good day. I finished all my work last night, got a good seven hours of sleep, and I'm headed out to Joshua Tree National Park. You can quote me on this: Any day in Joshua Tree is a good day.

Joshua Tree is special. It's a desert area and from a quick glance it doesn't seem like much. I mean, it's "just" desert. But when you're there, and not for very long, you start to see things and feel things, metaphysical things that make you look more. And more there is. The longer you stay the more aware you become, the more you feel, the more you *see*. It's its own religion. And it continues when you get home and look at your photos. You discover all sorts of things in the wild rock formations that you hadn't noticed before: faces of old wise men, giant eagles and ancient amphibians. Shadows of holiness.

I kick The Beast into first gear, take off and it happens again, like it does every time. The very moment I start a ride, even before I get out of my driveway, a mix of freedom and adventure rushes through me. After I settle into the freeway flow of Interstate 210 East, I reflect back and think I first felt that freedom-rush when I first learned to crawl. I felt it more when I first learned to walk and run. But when I first learned to ride a bicycle, that freedom-rush multiplied exponentially. And the more I felt that freedom, the more I wanted it, and the more I rode. It wasn't long before I was limitless.

As with almost everyone else, my two-wheeled life began with riding a bicycle, though I don't know exactly how old I was when the training wheels came off. I loved riding bicycles every time I went anywhere, that childhood thrill of wild-eyed discovery. My mom came to depend on me to ride down Westcott Street and across Lovers Lane to the Stop 'n' Shop grocery store (even though it was small, it had its own butcher) and get whatever we needed for dinner. I disliked being asked because I was always doing something else that was, of course, much too important to be interrupted. Nevertheless, I always enjoyed the ride itself, as short as it was.

Before puberty, before I even knew what puberty was, a new kind of bicycle came out called the Stingray. It was a small bike with only one gear but they had an appealing, sporty look, the revolutionary banana seat, and were painted bright colors. The most appealing thing about them, however, was that they were tailor-made for doing wheelies. A few kids in the neighborhood got one as soon as they were available and they immediately became the envy of everyone else. I wanted one. Desperately. I wanted to do wheelies. Desperately. The desperation to get my own Stingray grew with each day as Christmas approached. I needed a new bike anyway, my parents agreed, so I set about leaving Stingray hints whenever I could. (We didn't do Christmas lists back then.)

I was born in America but my parents were Danish, from the old country itself, as were my brother and sister. I never learned to read, write or speak Danish because my dad wanted us to be Americans, pure and proud. But there were old country views that permeated our home and one of them was about bicycles. Bicycles were a practical matter and a practical matter only. And banana seats, bright colors and wheelies are not practical. According to my Danish-minded parents, the best bicycles were the ones that would last a lifetime or two, weighty things that could crush an armored vehicle. So when Christmas Eve came (we opened presents on the night of Christmas Eve, a Danish tradition) I found myself the owner of a brand new, capable-of-crushing-an-armored-vehicle, last-a-lifetime-or-two, won't-do-wheelies bicycle from Sears.

I was aghast. Almost tearful. I decided right then and there that it was the ugliest thing ever made. But my parents were beaming. After all, they had gotten me the best bicycle money could buy. I did my best to feign enthusiasm and rode around for a while so they could see how thrilled I was. The thing is, even though I honestly tried, I never came to like that bicycle. Doing wheelies was impossible, it was an odd, boring white and was so heavy I could barely lift it. The thing is, though I truly disliked that bicycle, I always enjoyed the riding itself – the wind in your hair and the freedom and all that – but was always a little embarrassed around the other kids who were doing wheelies on their Stingrays. Perhaps this was when and why I came to do most of my riding alone. Several years later, my two-wheeled life pretty much ended for a while. Tired of suffering the ignominy of a Sears bicycle that wouldn't do wheelies, I had been leaving it at school off and on for a few months hoping someone would steal it. Finally, someone did.

I'm on Interstate 210 East passing by the cities of Pasadena, Arcadia, Azusa, Glendora, San Dimas and Rancho Cucamonga. Despite the fairly thick traffic, we're all moving along at the speed limit or a little faster. My personal safety radar is on so I occasionally change lanes or slow down or speed up a tad but nothing out of the ordinary comes my way. One interesting thing is that this safety radar doesn't diminish the freedom-rush at all. For me, at least. However, I'll admit that the adventure level isn't that high, but that's the nature of riding in thick traffic when your safety radar is on, as it should be.

My thoughts go back to my two-wheeled history and I remember my first motorcycle ride. I was around thirteen years old when my brother-in-law, Robert, bought a Honda 250. Good guy that he was, he decided to teach me how to ride. (I smile as I remember how I enjoyed saying his full name: Harry Lester Robert Scott.) We stood in the shade of our fruitless mulberry tree in the front yard as he carefully explained how a motorcycle is controlled, particularly how you shift gears. This was a couple of years after my dad had taught me to drive a stick shift in his red Ford Falcon (three-speed on the column, baby!) so, in theory, I understood what he was saying. On the other hand, I couldn't grasp the idea of working the clutch with my left hand instead of my left foot, and shifting with my left foot instead of my right hand. But instead of admitting I didn't think I could ride his Honda (couldn't bring myself to do that) I convinced Robert it wouldn't be a problem.

He rolled it into the street, I mounted up and took off with the hope that all that motorcycle riding technique would come to me in a flash, especially the part about shifting gears. It didn't. I stayed in first gear but continued to roll on the throttle. I looked at the speedometer and I was doing 25 mph; that little engine must have been whining at over a hundred decibels. I'm halfway down the block when all of my attention goes to this small dog that's chasing me on my right. Unaware, I wandered to the left and ended up sideswiping an old, beat up DeSoto sedan. Robert had the wisdom to not let me ride his Honda anymore.

I was in my mid-thirties when I took my second motorcycle ride. I was helping some friends move out to Perris, a hilly, sparsely populated area about seventy miles southeast of Los Angeles. Their new neighbors, who were also helping with the move, pulled out a few dirt bikes toward the end of the day and took turns riding them up and down the hills, which had a few trails on them but were mostly dirt, gravel and weeds. They asked if I wanted to take a ride. Despite still knowing nothing about operating a motorcycle, and remembering my first ride, I said I would love to. (I still couldn't bring myself to admit not knowing how.) I took off down the hill. I still couldn't reckon with the shifting of gears so I never got out of first, but the hill was steep enough that I kept gaining speed. Not far from the bottom I knew I was in trouble because if I kept going straight I was going to end up slamming into some nasty bushes. I made a right turn, immediately began sliding on the gravel and went down on the low side, badly scraping my right foot, leg and hand.

My third ride was even more harrowing. My buddy, Vic, had two bikes, a Kawasaki Vulcan Nomad 1500 and a Yamaha V-Star 650, which he used for commuting. He wanted a different commuter bike and one day asked if I wanted to buy his Yamaha. I declined the offer but couldn't get the idea of riding a motorcycle out of my head. For my whole life, whenever I saw someone riding, I'd imagine how wonderful it must be. But for some reason, I could never translate that image onto myself. In other words, when it came to riding my own motorcycle, there was an ever-present stop sign in my mind.

Vic persisted. He kept telling me about his rides and how great it feels and how much fun it all is. Finally, some months later, I agreed to check out the Yamaha. These were his entire instructions.

That's the throttle.

That's the front brake.

That's the rear brake.

That's the clutch.

That's the shifter; down for 1st, up for 2nd, 3rd, 4th and 5th.

Neutral is between 1st and 2nd.

Ah! Simple! Easy! I climbed on the bike and my first thought was how big it was, which lowered my confidence considerably. My plan was to angle to the right out of the driveway, go to the end of the block, turn around and come back. Simple! Easy! But as the front wheel crossed the gutter I realized I didn't have a clue as to what I was doing. Again, I was in trouble and knew it. The back tire had just crossed the gutter when something caught my eye. It was probably the sun reflecting off a window of the house across the street, but I panicked. What if it's a car? I meant to brake but, instead, rolled hard on the throttle. I shot across the street, went over the curb, ran over one of those green plastic boxes the cable companies put up, side-swiped a seven-foot hedge, went over the side of a brick-lined flower bed, and finally stopped when my head hit the bricks on the other side. I had a slight concussion, there was a dent on the bottom side of the gas tank and gas was spilling onto my jeans.

It was the dent in the gas tank that did it. For sixty thousand miles, Vic had kept that bike in pristine condition and it took me less than sixty feet to ruin it. I couldn't stand the thought of my buddy trying to sell a bike with a dent in the gas tank (he'd have to come down on the price) so I figured it was up to me to buy it. It was the only honorable thing to do. I signed up for a motorcycle safety course but I had to wait six weeks before there was an opening. I had planned to go back to Vic's and learn how to shift gears and brake but never did.

Right after San Bernardino, which is about halfway to Joshua Tree, the 210 heads southeast and later becomes Interstate 10. About twenty-five miles later, the I-10 starts going straight east and not long after the Morongo Casino there's a sight that's never good news for bikers. Windmills. Rows and rows of them. (It's called the San Gorgonio Pass Wind Farm but a more apt name would be the San Gorgonio Wind Bombardment.) There's a simple reason windmills are planted where they are and it's because there's a lot of wind, and a lot of wind is never pleasant for two-wheeled travelers. However, sometimes, like today, I look at it as a way to sharpen my skills with The Beast. There is a freedom in being able to competently handle your motorcycle, or anything for that matter, and it is a high joy. In high winds like this, it becomes a high adventure as well.

I survive the wind bombardment and afterward go back to reminiscing about my two-wheeled adventures. It was during the motorcycle safety course that I first realized what motorcycling was *really* about. One of the instructors was a good guy, helpful and conscientious. The other one, Mr. I'm-Awesomely-Important, was a run-of-the-mill tin god who yelled his instructions in an awesomely important way and would mock and laugh at anyone who made a mistake.

My first day of riding was torture. I got serious heat exhaustion, I could barely see or think, and all the while my eardrums were abused by Mr. I'm-Awesomely-Important, though I was never the direct target of his contempt. That night, I had excruciating cramps in my legs and a headache that put me in the fetal position. I felt better the following day and so did everyone else. In fact, the group was even a bit cheerful. But that made Mr. I'm-Awesomely-Important yell his awesomely important instructions even more loudly.

I believe it was the second to last exercise. We had to ride about sixty yards doing various things that we'd learned to do in other exercises. Once we got to the end, we were to make a wide left turn then ride back to where we started and get in line. I don't remember the exact maneuvers we did but I do remember Mr. I'm-Awesomely-Important yelling that on the way back we were *not* to shift into third gear; no one was permitted to go past second gear and if he caught anyone in third gear he'd kick them out of the class and they wouldn't get a refund. I did the maneuvers fairly well, sort of, made my left turn, and was riding back when I heard, again, Mr. I'm-Awesomely-Important berate someone. Something clicked inside of me and I shifted into third gear.

It was a small defiance, to be sure, but a defiance nonetheless. At that moment, on a small 250cc Kawasaki Eliminator going maybe 25 mph for all of thirty yards, it hit me. The wind, the freedom, the excitement. If Mr. I'm-Awesomely-Important kicked me out of the class, fine. He'd forever lost his influence and I'd learn to ride anyway. Fortunately, he never did notice that I went into third gear so I stayed in the class.

However, I failed the final test. We were given points, the higher the number, the worse you did. I think the passing grade was something like seventeen or eighteen. I got twenty-nine, tied for the worst. The helpful and conscientious instructor took me and the other twenty-nine-pointer aside and suggested that maybe we shouldn't become motorcyclists. It was an understandable suggestion said in a civil way, but it didn't stick. From just that seconds-long feeling of freedom, I had made up my mind that I was going to ride no matter what. I had six months to come back and pass the final test but decided that I would pass it the following weekend.

The next day, Vic brought over the Yamaha, my bike now, and for the next week I practiced and practiced some more, never going out of the neighborhood. In the first three days, I went down five times. There was a gash on my left leg, my hip was out of joint and my clothes smelled like gasoline. I also got into my first almost-accident.

A guy in an old Cadillac the size of an oil tanker backed out of a driveway without looking in his rearview mirror or turning his head. I stopped with only a foot to spare. Fortunately, I had remembered something the helpful and conscientious instructor said: Always assume you're invisible. Good advice because I *was* invisible to that guy in the oil tanker Cadillac.

I kept at my practicing, still never ventured out of the neighborhood, and managed to stay upright for the next three days. That Sunday I went back to the motorcycle safety class and when I got on the 250cc bike, I couldn't believe how small it was and how easy it was to handle compared to my bike. I passed with a score of nine.

It wasn't long after I began riding that I wrote the anthem at the beginning of this book. In fact, I wrote it the very evening I got home after my first multi-day ride. I liked it then and I still like it now because it echoes that primal freedom I experience while riding, a freedom I'd always longed for.

Ever since my wife, Rosemary, had passed away I had been looking, at times waiting, for something. Something to do, something to be, just *something*. I couldn't articulate what need or desire that that something would fill but I knew it would be the proverbial missing puzzle piece in my life. I wasn't looking to replace Rosemary, nothing could do that, but her passing made me realize that there was a vacancy in my own personal life. Truly, the dead and the dying give us many gifts and this was one of hers.

I tried all sorts of things, many were fun, but none of them really did it for me. Until those thirty yards of riding in third gear. I knew right then that riding a motorcycle was that "something" I had been looking for because it perfectly fulfilled the longing I had had for the freedom I'd lost along with my Sears bicycle, a longing I may never have realized had it not been for Rosemary. Hers was the soft passion that changed my destiny.

For what seemed like my entire life, I'd had a mild suspicion and distrust of bikers, which didn't make sense because I'd never experienced any kind of hassle from one. Nevertheless, every time I met one, or even just saw one on the street, that suspicion and distrust would quietly creep into my thoughts. This caused a small conflict in me because at the same time I had a deep wish to again experience the freedoms of riding. The evening after graduating the motorcycle safety course, I took a long look at the attitudes I had harbored concerning bikers. I tracked it back and back and finally came to a time when I was about six years old.

I had had it inculcated into me that bikers were either evil drug pushers, merciless gun runners, pill-popping stink-holes, back-stabbing thieves or all of the above, and from the moment anyone got on a motor-cycle, they were forever following a path to becoming those things. (Gee, thanks Mom!) I'd long since forgotten that I'd been given those views but during all those intervening years, I was unknowingly subject to them. Now, had I ever actually *looked* at this absurdity, I would have easily seen that it was just that: absurd. But I never did look because nothing had ever happened in my life that would have gotten me to look. Until Rosemary passed which led to the day when I shifted into third gear and defied the threats of an authority figure. I had finally discovered the source of that ever-present stop sign in my mind that had for years kept me from the freedoms of riding.

For a while I regretted all those lost years of riding enjoyment but coming out of that regret was simple. I just rode every day. The freedoms of riding fifteen to twenty thousand miles a year will make any regret disappear.

In a larger context, the very fact that I was riding a motorcycle was a defiance, a defiance against those absurd notions I got when I was a kid and a defiance against all those who harbor and cling to those notions. (Except for my mom. Even though she's no longer with us, defying her doesn't feel right so with her, I defy only the notions.) In the beginning, one of those I was defying was myself, or more accurately, my past-self. It was my past-self I was defying because riding had changed me. I had become a different man. It wasn't a complete change, of course, but it was big enough that I felt new and expansive, free to be something that some people consider lower caste. I had finally broken the chains of a hidden intolerance.

The wide margins of my life had considerably narrowed.

In the months afterward, I rode every day, sometimes in the canyons, sometimes on the freeway, sometimes on both. I wasn't obsessed with it, but I soon came to rely on it to break away from the disappointments, dol-drums and dissonances of life. I'd ride to the edge of my neighborhood, stop alongside the road and decide: Left or right? East or west? Canyon or freeway? I'd choose one then go, and it didn't matter which one I chose. Within minutes I'd experience a type of freedom similar to the one I'd experienced in the motorcycle safety course. It's a getting-away freedom, the kind you get when you escape from an unwanted situation, like leaving a low-paying job or ending a "friendship" with someone who talks behind your back. If you ride, this getting-away freedom is always within reach; you just go out and ride. You ride for a while and pretty soon, all those things that were pushing you down are gone.

I turn off Interstate 10 and make my way north on Highway 62. I'm excited. Joshua Tree pulls that out of me. I cut loose all of my recollections and what remains is freedom and how utterly good it is to have it flow through me and with me. In a way, though, it's odd because there's nothing I'm getting away from, nothing I need to defy; everything in my life is rolling along just fine: my work, my family, my friends. There is a complete lack of dissonance. So what, I wonder, is the nature of this freedom I'm now experiencing? It's new, it feels different, and it doesn't fit into the mold of breaking-away freedom. Where is it coming from and how did it come about?

Just before Morongo Valley, I lean hard into the sweepers on the 62, The Beast's suspension hunkers down and my speed is infinite. I work my way through the traffic and traffic lights in Yucca Valley and make a right on Park Boulevard, which wigwags its way to the Joshua Tree entrance. Inside the park, I ride for a bit just looking at Mother Nature's rock sculptures, which are all-satisfying. I think again of this new freedom and realize what it is: it's a *going-to* freedom. I'm not "getting away," I'm "going to." Today it's the splendid environment of Joshua Tree, but it could have been anything from learning how to dance ballet to going to a tavern and having a tall, cold mug of beer.

I pull into a lonely spot, hike up between the rocks for a ways and come to a small flat area. Far below, The Beast is gleaming in the sunlight and standing guard. A few birds rush overhead, the wind is quiet, and the air is flawless. I gaze over the mystical desert. It's here that I realize another freedom. A freedom that's not the result of "getting away" or "going to." It's the limitless and magical world of Freedom itself. No adjectives, no qualifiers. FREEDOM. It's the feeling that you can be anything, do anything, have everything simply because you want to. I am untethered.

17

THE GOLDEN LADY

Perfection is my lifelust. All my life, I've looked for it, admired it, dreamed about it and worked toward it. Perfection is something you can work on at any time no matter what you're doing, from building a temple to Buddha to frying up some hash browns. Even sleeping. And if you always keep it in mind, the things you do, the things you create will be better for it. Truly, the moment you adopt the philosophy of "good enough," you're on that dusty road to a mediocre dead end.

The path to Perfection is a divine frustration. Frustrating because there is always at least one flaw in what we do and create, though sometimes it's unnoticeable. But the frustration doesn't matter because the divine nature of Perfection is such that the road to it is flawlessly satisfying. Allow me an apology to Keats and Grecian Urns everywhere: Though I agree that Truth is beautiful, it is Perfection that is Beauty itself.

An easy day. That's what I'm thinking as I finally, and a bit reluctantly, ease out of the canyons just north of Los Angeles and onto the boulevard. And it had been an easy day. I had easily navigated around the patches of bad road, sand and water, hadn't taken any turns too widely or had to brake too quickly. Scraped the pegs a few times but that's just fun. All day, the clouds had languished and cool breezes had laced the warm air. It was one of those days, one of those easy days, where you own the road and the friendly earth on which it rests.

One wonderful thing about living in the area where I do is that there are so many great canyons to ride. When I woke up this morning and looked out the window, my first thought was that today is a perfect day to ride one of those canyons, which is something I think most mornings. The canyon I know better than any other is Little Tujunga (tuh-HUNG-guh), the south entrance of which is only a mile from my house. The 15.9 miles from stop sign to stop sign are my personal slice of heaven and I know it better than any other road because I've ridden it more than any other, at least a hundred times. The main reason I like it is because it's not easy to negotiate, which means it's the perfect place to work toward perfecting your skills. It offers every kind of challenge any biker could need: varying qualities of road surfaces, decreasing radius turns, blind corners, hairpins galore, banked turns, off-cambered turns, and some S-turns that'll put a smile on anyone's face; all the while avoiding sand and gravel and road kill with fifty to three hundred foot cliffs to one side or the other.

The traffic is always sparse to non-existent as it twists its way through Angeles National Forest and past the Wildlife Waystation, which sits on 160 acres. The north summit (there are two summits) is Bear Divide and there's a sign that says it's a picnic area. I suppose you could call it that. There are two tables, a trashcan and a small area of grass but no bathroom. Those two tables and a trashcan are all the amenities you'll find on the entirety of Little Tujunga, which is one reason there's so little traffic. But it does have an incredible view. Far below is Santa Clarita and farther north is the theme park Magic Mountain, which is home to several world-class roller coasters.

One some-day-you-gotta-check-this-out side trip starts at Bear Divide and goes west on the narrow, but paved, Forest Route 3N17, also known as the Santa Clara Truck Trail. About three miles up is a mountain fire station and about a mile after that it dead-ends at a plain white building with high windows. Park wherever you can, then walk up the little trail around the right of the building for maybe fifty yards and you'll come to a soaring, 360 degree view of the mountains and the San Fernando Valley that you'll want to savor for hours.

However, today I pass that side road and continue my present hankering which is to hard-slam the curves of Little Tujunga. Not far past the second bridge, there's a dip where a small stream sometimes crosses the road. Right there is a road sign I've never seen anywhere else and it always gives me a little chuckle: ALGAE MAY BE PRESENT. For the last few miles, beginning when you cross Placerita Canyon, the name changes to Sand Canyon and the road straightens up. It's a shady, ranch-style home neighborhood and the perfect length of road to catch your breath while the adrenalin level settles down.

I pass over the 14 Freeway and make a quick right onto Soledad (SO-luh-dad) Canyon. Soledad is not a straight road either but it's far from being the challenge that Little Tujunga is. I like that it's not heavily trafficked even on the few miles next to some Santa Clarita neighborhoods, after which there are no stop signs for about eighteen miles. It's mostly shaded, passes some old railroad cars, goes through a tunnel, and passes by the small town of Acton, where there's a great place to eat called Crazy Otto's, the walls of which are covered with license plates from all over the United States. After Acton, Soledad merges with the Sierra Highway and becomes treeless and pretty straight. However, the good news is that because you're on the south side of the elevated 14 Freeway, you're shielded from the brutal winds that oftentimes blow through there.

At the outskirts of Palmdale, I turn right onto Angeles Forest Highway, which takes me back into Angeles National Forest. Soon afterward it starts getting interesting, ride-wise and view-wise, and it just gets better and better. And better and better. After around twenty-five miles (not sure of the exact distance because the views are so fetching I always forget to check the odometer), I make a left on Upper Big Tujunga Canyon, which is like the entrance to paradise: nothing but sweepers, no stop signs, no yield signs, very little traffic and exemplary mountain views. The speedometer seldom dips under 50 mph, and I never have to brake. After nine miles it dead-ends and I make a left onto the legendary Angeles Crest Highway.

Now we're talking. If Upper Big Tujunga is the entrance, Angeles Crest IS paradise. Perfectly banked turns one after another, hardly a straightaway, the road like #1 grit sandpaper, my hair slapping in the wind, vast and gloriously inspiring views, crystalline air, and in the span of about twenty miles the altitude goes from three thousand to over seven thousand feet. It's like you're riding a roller coaster and running on jet fuel. I ride all the way up to the summit, get off my bike, breathe in the atmosphere, relish the hum in my body, and take a long look at Heaven itself.

I backtrack down Angeles Crest, stop at Newcomb's Ranch for a lemonade, backtrack down Upper Big Tujunga, take a left on Angeles Forest and five miles later make a right on Big Tujunga Canyon, which is a cross between its two siblings: the twisties of Little Tujunga and the sweepers of Upper Big Tujunga. It's always a thrill to ride over that bridge, which feels like it's a thousand feet high. Eventually, I'm in the town of Sunland, a community on the upswing. As I ride through the neighborhoods, I think of my route. Over 150 miles of the purest canyon riding you'll find anywhere, and all the while I saw fewer than three dozen cars. Yep, "Heaven" *is* an apt description.

Dusk. I pull into the Jack-in-the-Box on Foothill Boulevard. Between the parallel parking and the diagonal parking are two triangular spaces; one surrounded by a cement curb, the other a no-parking space. I park in the no-parking space then walk in and get my dinner: an Ultimate Cheeseburger, fries and a root beer. The curbed triangle is covered with soft grass and a few rocks, one of which is perfectly sized and shaped for a nice sitting, and that's where I enjoy my meal. Easy. Easy and convenient.

I finish dinner. The air has grown a little heavy but the cool of the late day is making itself known so it's still comfortable. I turn to my right and watch a woman on a bicycle ride over and stop about five feet in front of me. Far on the other side of her the sunset begins to mingle blues and yellows. My new companion stands in profile, staring straight to my left, talking rapidly, as if to an impatient confessor. At first I can't understand her but after a minute or so my ears adjust so I can make out the words, which are completely unrelated: car-when-pills-stop-stop-kids…. I watch and listen. After a minute or so, she dismounts, looks for a place to park, and sees me for the first time. She stops talking and stares, her eyes iris-less and deep, then after some moments resumes her babbling and nervous search.

I take a close look at my bicycled companion. Her skin is embedded with grime in large, out-of-focus blotches, like black ink on wet paper. Her tattered clothes are mismatched and she wears an old hat. Alternately, she wrings her hands and flails her arms in erratic arcs. Frantically she babbles non-stop: where-can't-word-I-please-please…. Too, the bicycle is old and rusted and covered with grime and soot; the basket on the front of it is filled with junk as unrelated as the words she speaks.

I point to a space behind my bike and tell her she can park the bicycle there. Again she stops talking and stares, her mouth slightly open. She parks her bike and again resumes her droning, disjointed narrative. She paces back and forth. Birthday-dark-meds-don't-slow…. . She starts for the door then comes back. After she repeats the routine, I offer to watch her bike while she goes inside to get something. Again, she freezes and her eyes gaze. She goes inside.

I hear a clank then the buzz of neon lights firing up, which give the dusk an odd tint, as if I'm sitting in a shaded, watercolored scene. I think about the day, the blessings of an easy ride, the liberties of riding a motorcycle. Again I take in the sunset and my thoughts go to the constancies of life: the blue sky and the meandering clouds, the faithful sun and the turning stars, the winds and the sounds of the winds. The noise of the traffic on the boulevard offers an ironic tranquility. A '67 Camaro rumbles by.

A few minutes later my companion comes out with two plastic cups of ice water. She gives me one and I offer a genuine thank you. To me, it's significant. Significant because, despite her deteriorating state, despite her wildly scattered thoughts, despite her pauperized life, she had thought to repay me for watching her bicycle. She continues her frenetic manner, never once sipping any water. I take a drink and watch and wait and wonder what had happened to her, what sequence of occurrences had led to this woman, who at one time, I determine, was quite pretty, living a dirty and homeless existence.

I wonder what those eyes had seen. Are they actually bottomless and without comprehension or does their darkness hide shunted dreams and lost joys? What had she wanted to be? What had she been? What had she accomplished? It's clear, to me at least, that her present state is an unnatural one, that it had been purposefully caused. I imagine those who had caused it and come up with too many dark possibilities. Ultimately what lies heavily is the tragedy. The tragedy of a woman, a pretty and productive woman, degraded and dirtied into an ownerless slave. The sunset darkens, yellow to orange, blue to indigo.

She goes to her bicycle and stands in a state of confusion as to what to do with her cup of water, so I offer to throw it away. Again she stops and gazes, again I wonder what lies deep in those eyes. She hands me her cup and, along with mine, I throw it in the trashcan to my right. When I turn around, she has backed out her bicycle, set it on the kickstand and is madly rummaging through the basket on the front of it. She finds what she wants, grasps it fervently, then solemnly presents it to me with both hands.

It's a small, orange rubber frog with a small hole in the mouth where there had once been a plastic squeaker. An old bathtub plaything or a pet dog's toy. Another gift. I'm warmed by her consideration for me and her willingness to repay even the smallest favor. I thank her again and smile. She gets on her bicycle and rides away to my right but instead of exiting the parking lot, she turns left and rides around the outside of the drive-through. When she gets straight across from me, about thirty yards away, she stops and looks directly at me one last time, her silhouette framed by the nearly-gone sunset. An invisible corridor connects us, devoid of sound and motion and time. As the last rays of the sunset disappear, she speaks in a clear and beautiful voice; calm, like a herald angel. She says, "I turn you into gold."

I turn you into gold. I sit for a long time pondering those words. Is it an ancient blessing? A line from some obscure song? A wish for prosperity? Detached and floating, I observe the goings-on around me, the easy flow of life as it were: people walking to and fro and their back and forth conversations, the opposite streams of traffic, a young man offering his milkshake to his sweetheart, she smiling and demure. Stars disappear and reappear as the clouds amble. I breathe deeply the fertile air and allow it to naturally escape my lungs. Somehow it all makes sense. There is, indeed, a rhythm and rhyme to the world. But what of the Golden Lady? Where does she fit in? What is the significance behind her golden proclamation? And why did she say it to me?

True, it could have all been happenstance, the constant uttering of disjointed words accidentally forming a sentence. It's a mathematical possibility, though quite remote, and, I suppose, it could have eventually occurred though it may have taken eons. But that doesn't seem right. I *had* felt that connection between us, that corridor, and she *had* spoken clearly and directly to me in a voice far different from before. No, the words were deliberate. There *was* a purpose behind her proclamation, a meaning, or perhaps many meanings. I sigh. The Golden Lady is gone along with the sunset, and I will never see either again.

I put the orange frog in my bag, get on my bike, push the starter and the engine roars. Another constant in my life. Before I travel that short road home, my last ride of the day, I pull out the orange frog and take another look. To the physical eye there is nothing remarkable about it. It's grimed and artless, and without the squeaker in its mouth it can't even fulfill its original, single intention. Had it not been for my bicycled companion, it would be nothing more than an insignificant piece of landfill. But there, in my hand, the gift from the Golden Lady is a priceless talisman. I carefully place it back in my bag and decide it will always accompany me wherever I ride.

I often think about the Golden Lady and her golden words. But as I write that, I realize that that's not truly accurate. You see, I don't actually think about them; rather, I view the memory, look into her eyes, hear her angelic voice and become blessed with the benign mystery.

I turn you into gold.

18

BACK HOME

Oftentimes, it's the little things, the snippets of life, that stay with us the longest, that we enjoy remembering the most. For me, one of them was in Bengough, Saskatchewan, Canada.

I'm standing there in the shade, outside the small Co-Op market, next to the displays of antifreeze, windshield washer and fertilizer, sipping the last of my Fanta Orange when I first see her. She casually sits on her bike, like it's what she was born to do. She rides into the parking lot like she owns it, puts her kickstand down right in front of the door and strides into the store, like she owns that, too. Five minutes later she comes out with a small bag filled with whatever and carefully tucks it away.

What a sight! Cute as a kitten in clover with blond pigtails under a pink and purple helmet, multi-colored tennis shoes and green socks rolled down to her ankles. The tires on her bike have pink sidewalls, streamers come out of the handgrips, and the sun shining on the chrome looks like million sparklers in a hall of mirrors. She fixes her eyes on me and I can barely breathe. She rides over and stops next to The Beast. I'm self-conscious about all the dirt. She slowly checks him out, front to back to front again. My heart is pounding. She bites her lip. I tag her at six years old, maybe seven, and figure her mom sent her to get something for supper. She looks up at me, head tilted, eyes squinting in the sunlight.

Cute-as-a-Kitten-in-Clover Girl With Blond Pigtails: Nice bike, mister!

Me: Thanks. Got a good-looking ride yourself.

She giggles and pedals away, pigtails bouncing in the breeze.

When bikers gather together, the many conversations and the opinions given on them vary as widely as the ways to describe a sunset, and if it weren't for having to sleep, they would never end. There is, however, one thing we all agree on, different bikes, personalities and ages notwithstanding: It's not about the destination, it's about the journey. It's become a well-known biker truism and is something that is true about all of life and is part of the non-biker philosophy as well.

I saw a major league baseball manager on TV years ago. He said the greatest feeling in the world was winning the World Series but losing a World Series was a close second. If you understand why that is, then you understand that the real joy, the real thrill, the real essence of riding a motorcycle and living itself *is* the journey, not the destination.

At some point, these conversations always come around to the reasons we ride. It's an interesting topic because there are as many reasons as there are riders, and they are all valid. Even with all these many different views on the subject, at some point there's one word, one concept, that always gets mentioned, and it's something that's apropos to anyone anywhere, rider or not.

In fact, it's so ingrained in all of us that it doesn't need to be taught or even mentioned, though it's mentioned often. Tomes have been written on it and will be written on it, though it defies analysis. When it's denied us, we demand it; when we have it, we want more, yet there is nothing about it that guarantees security or comfort or wealth. There is an unlimited supply of it and it costs nothing, yet its price is sometimes dear. Innumerable brave men and women, without regret, have died for it only to give it away.

It's in your attitude when you settle into an easy chair after the daily grind, or work three days straight just to get every detail perfect. It's confidently shaking hands with a new client even though you have holes in your socks and you're three months behind on your mortgage. It's in the level, friendly gaze when you say, "I'll be there," even though you know it's impossible, but you somehow get there anyway.

It's in the embrace when we say, "I love you." It's in the touch when we say, "It'll be okay." It's in the tears when we say, "We'll see each other again." You can hear it in the voice when someone says, "I'm writing a poem," or "I'm learning how to wind surf," or "I'm having ice cream for lunch." It's in the nod of a fellow biker headed in the opposite direction, in the sweat of six guys playing a pick-up basketball game, in the silent breaths of a sleeping child.

We see it in the paintings of Magritte, Degas, and Goya; in a child's crayon drawing taped to a refrigerator door. We read it in the lines of Conrad, Whitman, and Austen; in fantasy comics that take place on other worlds. We hear it in the music of Mozart, Beethoven, and Palestrina; in the improvisations by the guy playing sax on a busy street corner, rusted coffee can set out for donations.

It's in the sky, light or dark, and in all the clouds and stars it holds; it's in the wind and the raindrops, in the mountains and streams that ignore man's partitions, in the seasons that forever unfold, one into the next. It echoes from the past, is amplified in the present, and waits for us in the future. It's in our dreams; perhaps it *is* our dream. It is the very fiber of our hearts.

Then there are times. Times when it becomes so real that it reaches out and slaps you awake. You're alone, no one around for miles, watching the colors of the morning sky change from indigo to orange to yellow to blue. A hawk glides close to the ground and there's a gentle rustling in the trees, yet the stillness is unmolested. The grasses quiver. It's then, amid the retreating shadows, when you lean back and close your eyes, it's then that you feel it. You can *feel* the earth turn toward the faithful sun; she turns and, along with her sister planets, she circles the sun and you feel that, too. And together with countless stars you actually feel the revolving of the Milky Way as we all progress along our odyssey through the galactic pillars and beyond. For a while you ponder the destination, then realize that it doesn't really matter, does it? After all, it's just another ride.

Freedom.

ABOUT the AUTHOR

Foster Kinn (a.k.a. Dwight Mikkelsen) was born in the central valley of California. He is the son and brother of Danish immigrants, the father of three, the grandfather of two, and a widower.

He has been a professional musician and composer his entire adult life. He has arranged and orchestrated for many artists, including Quincy Jones, Barbra Streisand, Chicago, and Whitney Houston, and has worked on hundreds of films and TV shows. His primary love, however, is Classical music. His music has been performed by artists and groups all over the world including the Los Angeles Philharmonic Orchestra, the Civic Orchestra of Chicago, the Pittsburgh Pops and the Vienna Opera Orchestra.

He describes himself as "fundamentally a freedom guy, a Classical music composer and a not-too-bad raconteur, who feels there is never enough time to ride his motorcycle."

Invitation for more fun and freedom!

Follow me on the road!

If you love what you read in Freedom's Rush, you'll want to get up-to-the-minute travel blogs as I traverse the continental U.S. and Canada on The Beast.

I only sends emails from the road, but I'm happy to share. Go to **www.FosterKinn.com** or **www.FreedomsRush.net**. Sign up for emails and to receive notice of my blogs (something my publisher insists I do).

Oh, and you'll also get to see all the pictures that you read about as a bonus!

You know the saying: Keep the shiny side up and the rubber side down.

Love,

Invitation for more fun and freedom!